Surviving
Henry

Surviving Henry

Adventures in Loving a Canine Catastrophe

ERIN TAYLOR YOUNG

Revell

a division of Baker Publishing Group
Grand Rapids, Michigan

© 2014 by Erin Taylor Young

Published by Revell
a division of Baker Publishing Group
P.O. Box 6287, Grand Rapids, MI 49516-6287
www.revellbooks.com

Printed in the United States of America

Library of Congress Cataloging-in-Publication Data
Young, Erin Taylor.
   Surviving Henry : adventures in loving a canine catastrophe / Erin Taylor Young.
      pages cm
   ISBN 978-0-8007-2356-9 (pbk.)
   1. Dogs—Behavior—Anecdotes. 2. Human-animal relationships. I. Title.
SF433.Y68 2014
636.7—dc23   2014007665

15 16 17 18 19 20 21   8 7 6 5 4 3 2

In keeping with biblical principles of creation stewardship, Baker Publishing Group advocates the responsible use of our natural resources. As a member of the Green Press Initiative, our company uses recycled paper when possible. The text paper of this book is composed in part of post-consumer waste.

To the memory of Glen Leroy Young,
a humble giant in farmer's clothes.
1922–2013

Acknowledgments

I always thought my first book would be dedicated to my husband and sons, but the passing of my dear father-in-law compels me to go back a generation. Would my husband, my sons, and I be who we are without Glen's legacy of service, generosity, and love? He lived with a gleam in his eye and the light of Jesus in his heart, and he impacted not just his family but his entire community. Thank you, Glen.

To Alan, my long-suffering husband, who believes in me enough to pay for writing conferences, loves me enough to protect my writing time, and always, *always* encourages me to follow God's call on my life—I love you. You are my noble hero.

To my sons, Jacob and Jonathan, who love Henry and willingly became part of this story—I can't wait to see the stories God has for the rest of your lives. Love you guys!

Thanks to my parents, Darrell and Marjorie Taylor, who always made me feel like anything was possible, including this book. You're the best. Your love has been a pillar holding me up all my life.

To Ruth Young, my second mom and wife to Glen—they say behind every great man there stands a woman. You have a legacy every bit as significant as Glen's, and then some. Thank you for always making me feel like one of your own.

To Holly Smit—as both critique partner and friend you are a God-given treasure. How would this book have ever grown up without you? You push me to be ever so much more than I think is possible. Thanks for walking this road with me, for praying it with me too, and for believing in nuggets and nothing wasted.

To Karen Ball—that God paired us for this ride is a great and awesome wonder to me. Thanks for being a steady rock of wisdom and for digging into this manuscript with me. By God's grace I'm blessed to call you both agent and friend.

Thanks to my writing buddies at OCFW. You make me grow. Thanks especially to Robin Patchen, Regina Jennings, and Sharon Srock, who read and critiqued Henry's story way back when.

Thanks to Rene Gutteridge, friend, mentor, and super-genius writer, who taught me, encouraged me, and kindly informed me I was a humor writer.

To Steve Laube, pastor to so many, many writers—you have shaped my career more than you know. Thank you.

To those who've prayed me through this process—Judy Dancy, Sue Isaac, the Heritage Baptist Church prayer team, and a certain way-cool underground Sunday school class (you know who you are)—I'm forever grateful.

To the amazing publishing team at Revell—y'all are gifted. And you make this fun. Thanks for letting me join the team.

Thanks to the most excellent staff at the Patience S. Latting Northwest Library. I couldn't ask for better or more encouraging co-workers.

Thanks to Gayle Roper, teacher extraordinaire and wise counselor, who guided me in just the right direction at just the right time.

To Angel Soriano and the folks at K9 University—God bless you for loving Henry and all the other dogs that pass through your doors.

To my God and Savior—this is an astounding journey. You make water come from the rock and send manna in the desert. Soli Deo gloria.

Note: Some names of both people and animals have been changed, including Henry's true sire and dam (though I'm sure all their other offspring are perfectly normal).

Author's Note That You Probably Won't Read but I'm Going to Write Anyway So No One Sues Me

This is a true-life story, not a word-for-word transcription of our life with Henry. It's not like I run around with a digital recorder in my pocket. I'm reconstructing events and providing dialogue based on my memory of the gist of what happened to shape this into an experience you can share with me. Read this for what it is—my entertaining spin on the real-life predicaments Henry blunders into.

For the sake of story, I sometimes combine several conversations, characters, or events into one and do a little skippy-do through time. You don't care about the mundane details of my existence, so isn't it best that I spare you? Furthermore, this isn't a full account of the good and bad of Henry. Publishers balk at a 560,000-word epic. I mean, Tolstoy could get away with it, but my real-life *War and Peace* doesn't need that sort of elaboration.

For the sake of humor, allow me some comedic exaggeration here and there, and we're good to go.

Enjoy.

1

Our dog has special needs, the greatest being the need for a lobotomy. After that, he could use a good dose of Prozac. Add some Ritalin and he'd approach the vague semblance of a well-adjusted canine. Feels almost doable.

Except for his trail of freakish accidents and half-baked suicide attempts.

Sometimes I think if Henry—that's the dog—had ended up in a different family, we'd all be better off. Some combinations just don't mix. Take Mentos candy and diet cola. Put them together, and you get a carbonated geyser blowing your bottle cap.

Pets are supposed to be fun. A pleasant enrichment of your life. Dogs especially. Loving, loyal, sleeping by your feet.

Henry is the anti-dog.

I don't believe in divine misprints. But life with Henry makes me wonder.

Today, for instance, I find myself careening through my neighborhood at Mach 5, clinging to the handlebars of a wobbly, electric scooter tied to a brawny dog whose sole desire—I discover a bit too late—is to tow me pell-mell across the Yukon and back. Lemme tell ya, they don't make brakes strong enough for that.

Contrary to what you might believe, I did not wake up this morning and wish for death. I was simply implementing yet another wear-out-the-dog plan. Henry is a purebred boxer, a bundle of muscle who makes other high-energy dogs look comatose. We try to counteract his spirited enthusiasm—otherwise known as maniacal hyperactivity—with massive doses of exercise. Better behavior through exhaustion, and all that. But we never tire Henry enough to achieve one piddly bit of better behavior. Walks don't do it. I could hike until my feet blistered out of my sneakers, and Henry might consider panting. I, on the other hand, would need a skin transplant.

I've even taken up jogging to drain this dog's endless stamina. I'm not in horrible shape, but running with Henry is downright discouraging. Even for a boxer, he's lean and leggy with a gait that stretches forever. I huff beside him in a brisk jog, and he barely breaks out of a walk, which bugs me, so I keep speeding up until my tongue hangs out farther than the dog's. When we come back from our three-mile torture tour, I'm on the verge of cardiac arrest, while Henry's wondering when the real exercise starts.

Borrowing my son's electric scooter is my latest genius scheme. My kid can sail around on the thing like it's an extension of his limbs. Surely I can manage it.

The plan is to stand comfortably on this fully powered vehicle and, with a twist of my wrist, roll about the neighborhood while Henry trots alongside. No sweat.

Literally.

Sooner or later Henry will wear out. Well, I guess the scooter battery could go first, but I've given it a full charge. It ought to be good for a two-hour trek.

I step onto the parked scooter and wobble like a novice tightrope walker. It's been thirty-plus years since the fifth grade, when hanging ten on my skateboard was like breathing. As I wave around searching for my inner surfer dude, a hint of foreboding tingles in my gut.

I squash it—I am *not* too old for this. If I get rolling, my balance will magically wake from hibernation. Still, I tie the leash to the handlebars so I can keep both hands clamped to the grips. Can't be too careful.

I inhale a deep morning breath, sweep my gaze over the neighborhood hills, and pin my focus on Henry. "Are you ready to go for a walk?"

Henry runs his sniffer over the scooter and looks up at me, a wary expression creasing his velvety brown forehead.

"What? You don't like the scooter? You're not going to ride it. Just trot along beside it."

With one foot, I shove off, and my wrist gives an expert I-used-to-own-a-motorcycle twist to the throttle. The motorcycle was only twenty-plus years ago, so my wrist is more in the groove than my balance.

The scooter whines to life and the chain kicks in, jerking my head back and about ripping my grip from the handlebars. I don't have time to recover before Henry gets an earful of high-pitched motor squeal and breaks into an Olympic sprint.

Guess what? Henry can run way faster than the scooter manufacturer's recommended safe speed.

My hair whips in the wind, and my mouth freezes in a Dear-Lord-please-help-me grimace. I think I might be screaming too. In a parade of near misses, I whiz past a mailbox, a lamppost, a parked car. My eyelids alternate between popping wide in horror and squeezing tight to shut out the fast-forward-gone-awry view.

Every muscle under that dog's fur bulges with locomotive power. His flattened ears and reckless stride scream his burning need to escape the horrifying contraption eating ground behind him.

Futile, since I've fastened him to the scooter.

I consider my options, feeling like a disaster movie extra whose credit is going to read, "Dead Body."

I could leap off, perform a triple roll across the asphalt, and pop to my feet before I get a concussion.

What am I, the Bionic Woman? A fine fantasy that can jolly well remain in fifth grade.

I could stay the course and wait for the inevitable lamppost-to-the-face crunch.

That sounds like fun.

I'm back to the jumping-off plan, except Henry will simply keep running. It's not like dragging a motorized scooter as it clangs and tumbles through the streets would pose a challenge to Henry's drive train. After I scrape myself off the pavement, I'll still have to chase Henry and the scooter until he plumb wears out—probably five or six miles down the road. Then I'll have to explain to my son why his beautiful Christmas present we paid a small fortune for looks like it's been tossed off Mount Everest.

The scooter won't look any better with the lamppost-to-the-face strategy, but a few broken bones on dear old Mom might garner some sympathy from my son.

Not.

Either way, we're into buying a new scooter. And paying a hospital bill.

My life is passing before my eyes, along with dollar signs, when somehow Henry zips off the road, up a driveway, and onto some lush sod. The turf slows our progress enough for me to imagine I have a chance.

I crush the brake handle, leap off the floorboard, and kick into a mid-air sprint that keeps me upright when I hit the ground, saving me from a slew of sod up the nose. I take .03 seconds to marvel that my fancy maneuver won't leave me buried under a tombstone that says, "Stupidity killed her, poor sap."

I'm now in a running tug-of-war with Henry the Rampaging Beast, and a hedge of holly looms in our path. There's no way we're making it through that sucker without shredding skin. Worse, a solid brick house waits on the other side.

I dig my heels into the grass and manage to turn Henry. He veers straight for a river birch. A slightly better option, considering the hedge and the house and all, except it's a sturdy looking tree.

And did I mention the lovely boulders surrounding its trunk?

Time for my last stand. Aside from the torment of smashing into a boulder and crumpling myself around some nice lady's birch, it's the explanation to the nice lady (or 911 responders) that I'd hate most.

My sneakers gain purchase in the turf. With what I'm sure is God-given extra strength, I pull on the handlebars and finally wrangle Henry to a halt—shy of the boulders.

I tremble in the aftermath of exertion. Henry totters sideways a step or two, then swings his head around and eyes me with a "How did I get here?" look. It's as if his brain took a vacation for the past few minutes and didn't even send a postcard.

I glare right back into his gaze. "Are you *kidding* me? You don't remember nearly killing us both?"

He gives the scooter a vague, suspicious glance, shakes his floppy ears, and hits me with a perky look that says, "Hey, let's go for a walk."

We can't loiter in someone else's yard forever. "Oh, all *right*. Come on."

He gives me an "Oh boy, a walk, a walk, a walk!" look and skips at my side while I push the stupid scooter all the way home.

Welcome to a typical day of life with Henry.

How did we get stuck with this dog? It probably has something to do with my childhood. Almost everything does.

I'm just a twig of a girl—maybe six years old—when doggie longing begins, but in my family it's understood we can't have one. The reason why is never satisfactorily explained. We just can't.

We can have a fish tank, though. My dad gets one from some friend who doesn't want it anymore. A swell indication of the aquarium's excitement potential. Fish are included in the deal. They come in two kinds—dull black or pasty white.

Yay. A tankful of ugly fish.

Then one day I find a bird outside by the mailbox. He's a bright green splash in a sea of brown weeds. He doesn't fly away when my little footsteps come close. I eye him for a while, not brave enough to touch him. He could sink his beak into my finger. Maybe give me lice, or the plague or something. I'm a kid. What do I know?

I find a stick and ease it against his lower belly. He scrunches his eyes shut but doesn't take to the air. A little push of the stick forces him to choose between falling over backward or hopping on the twig. He chooses the twig.

Yay, me. I caught the bird.

I hustle to the house to show him off. I can't exactly walk inside with him, so I ring the doorbell. Two or three times. Maybe ten.

The bird sits on the stick and looks sick.

The door barely cracks open.

"Mom, look what I found! Can I keep him?"

Her gaze pins to the bird. "Where did you get that?"

"I found him by the mailbox."

She frowns as if I'm fibbing. Good grief, how in the world could a kid produce a live bird from nowhere? Did she think I'd stolen it? Secretly purchased it from a neighbor kid? I admit that did happen once with some baby ducks, but that's another story.

I put on my most earnest face. "I caught him by the mailbox."

The bird stays perched on the twig, occasionally scrunching his eyes as if by doing so he could make the whole world disappear.

"I think he's tame. Can we keep him?"

Mom still wears the dubious frown.

One of my sisters arrives—Nadine, my partner (and I think the instigator) in the baby duck fiasco. Her eyes get sparkly when she sees the bird. "Sandy has an old cage in her basement we could borrow. They used to have a bird, but it died."

Sandy—Nadine's best friend—lives right down the street.

A near "maybe" sweeps across Mom's face, then it's gone. "It probably belongs to someone, and it's just lost."

"Then we should keep him safe," I say. "He can't be a wild bird."

Nadine runs off to snag the birdcage before Mom can protest.

I peer at the bright green feathers. "I wonder what kind of bird he is?"

"It's a parakeet." Mom comes outside, a definite "maybe" in her tone. "I used to have one when I was little. His name was Peetie the Parakeet."

"Peetie. What a great name. I should call this one Peetie."

Before long, Nadine's back, a rusty cage swinging from her hand. "They said we could use it as long as we want."

I guide Peetie's twig into his new home and have to virtually peel him off the stick and onto the bar running across the cage. He looks like he might fall over and die. "I think he's happy in there."

Mom's still frowning. "You need to find out where he belongs."

Nadine's head bobs with enthusiasm. "I'll help her. We can go door-to-door."

I bring Peetie into the house. "Let's keep him safe while we go out looking. But if I can't find his owner, can I keep him?"

Mom sighs. "We'll see."

Ah, the magic words.

Door-to-door, as Nadine and I interpret it, allows for efficiency through careful consideration of options. "There's the Wilmington house." I point at a white two-story. "I don't think they have birds, do you?"

"No. What about the Abbotts?"

"Nah. But we should ask at the Hills' house. They know a lot of people."

"Yeah. And I think someone who used to take piano lessons over at that blue house said they had birds there . . ."

After our not-very-thorough search, Peetie's owner remains a mystery. My parents let me keep him, probably figuring he's one feather short of the grave.

For some inexplicable reason, he survives. I have high hopes he can be the new best friend I'm longing for.

He sits in his cage and poops.

Ranks right up there with the fish.

But one day Nadine and I scrape together enough pennies to buy a hamster. This is allowed—I don't know why.

I'm pretty sure the whole plan is another brainchild of Nadine's, helped along by my disappointment in Peetie the Pooper. I yearn for a less aloof companion. It doesn't sink in that a pin-headed rodent with a life span of one thousand days isn't much to count on.

We name our hamster Cheetoe, and she does nothing but chew on the metal bars of her cage every night, rattling and shaking them so hard she might one day rip them out.

I learn the meaning of *nocturnal*.

Once in a while she runs a 12K on her squeaky wheel, just to change the music.

No wonder I have insomnia.

When she dies, we replace her with another hamster, because apparently I'm not that bright. In my defense, the lure of a cool new Habitrail cage, with all its sleek plastic tubes, suckers me in. I want to live there myself. I'm pretty sure McDonald's PlayPlaces were invented by someone who once owned a Habitrail.

The new hamster—Buffy—is a puffy beige thing that spends 99 percent of her time sleeping. We feed her, clean her cage, and let her out to run every now and then. Somehow, this is enough for Nadine.

I'd really rather have a dog.

Once in a while, something miraculous sprouts from seeds of affliction. Just when I'd given up on ever cuddling alongside a fireplace (which we didn't have) with a cozy, adoring dog (which we couldn't have), my oldest sister's former boyfriend—aka Rotten Ex—takes to hurling rocks at our house.

His first sortie breaks the outer glass of our large picture window and mars the inner glass. Granted, we can't prove Rotten Ex is the culprit, but a neighbor sees a person matching his description flee the scene.

He times his second attack for a dark night shortly after my parents replace the glass. Nadine and I are home alone, and the sharp crack of the assault shatters our security. Our little hearts gallop out of control until our parents come home.

The window hasn't broken, but an ugly scar, smack in the center, defaces it. My folks don't bother replacing the glass. Good thing, because long about midnight on the Fourth of July, Rotten Ex comes to terms with physics.

He chooses a brick. It lands on our living room floor.

The next day my dad buys a dog magazine to read up on breeds—guard-dog breeds.

Hooray for Rotten Ex! I forgive him, pretty much, for scaring me senseless.

I'm smart enough to keep this sentiment to myself, and I don't ask any questions. None of us kids do. Probably the first time in history a father occupies a house with silent daughters. Hopeful-dog-owner daughters.

A few days later we're at a boxer breeder's house. She has a lot of dogs, but only one for sale. He's elegant, sculpted muscle over the most agreeable of souls.

He visits each one of us, approaching with his ears perked in curiosity and his nose collecting a polite sniff. We all respond with a nice scritch-scratch of his silky coat. All except my mom. Her reluctant pat says, "I don't want to like you. This isn't my idea."

News flash: Mom hasn't boarded the dog-owner train. This could all derail.

The breeder leans back in her chair like she's getting comfortable for a good long chat. "What questions can I answer?"

She and Dad launch into a discussion that I don't pay attention to. Not until I hear the breeder say something about competitions.

"He's won several ribbons." She gestures to a trophy shelf behind her. "I have them over there with my other dogs' trophies. I guess you could say he's retired, though, since I don't show him . . ."

My lips form a big O. A pile of shiny hardware lights up her wall of fame. Trophies, ribbons, certificates—I've never seen anything like it. How beyond cool to have a real live show dog! Not that we'll show him. We don't know a thing about it. But we can totally brag to all the neighborhood kids. Oh, how I ache to get him.

"What exactly is his name?" Dad studies the dog. "I think you've called him a couple different things."

The breeder answers with a long string of multisyllable, foreign-sounding names that culminates in "Aaron."

My family bursts out laughing, and every gaze swings to me.

"Aaron?" Nadine's tone rings with the possibility of perpetual teasing. "That's his name?"

It's never good to share a moniker with the family dog. Is this going to be my personal torment in the deal? Can I live with that?

The dog trots over to the breeder and sits at her feet. She pets him with hands of well-practiced love. "Actually, I've taken to calling him Hank Aaron because he reminds me of the baseball player."

A collective sigh seems to escape the whole family. Okay, probably it's just me. Still, it feels like something clicks into place. The look on my dad's face says, "Hank . . . yes, I can live with that."

I look over at Mom. She wears an I-just-don't-know-about-this frown. My gut twists.

At that moment, Hank trots over to her, sits down, and puts his head in her lap. Then he hits her with doe eyes that say, "Please love me."

We come home with the dog.

Rotten Ex makes one last assault on our house. My folks throw open the door when they hear a thud on the siding. (Rotten Ex has rotten aim.) Hank charges outside and storms around the yard, barking a throaty challenge. We never see Rotten Ex again.

Like icing on our family cake, Hank is the sweetness, the flair that completes the dish. He comes housebroken and never tries to piddle on Mom's giant indoor plants. He doesn't eat a single toy, shoe, or piece of furniture. The boundaries of our yard become sacred to him, even though we don't have a fence.

The dog is the epitome of easy. I don't know why my parents say dogs take work. He sits on my feet, rests his head in my lap, and can't get enough of hanging-out togetherness. He gets the last lick of my ice cream bars and the first toy at Christmas. He plays on my schedule—meaning, whenever I feel like it—and never bugs me when I want to laze around reading. He sleeps by my bed every night and guards me from hatchet murderers. He chases snowballs in winter and a basketball he can't get his teeth around in summer. He lets me dress him in silly outfits and take picture after picture. I love him with all the love my kiddie heart can give.

He's there for my eighth-grade graduation party, high school too. He sends me off to college and grows old while I'm not looking.

One summer I come home, and he isn't there to greet me.

I never got to say good-bye.

2

Hank was my childhood model of dog perfection, playing the starring role in my true-love dog experience. Then I grow up, and along comes Henry, unabashed blemish on the canine community.

The circumstances surrounding Henry's birth portend greatness . . . er, uniqueness . . . okay, trouble.

His creator? God. But let's talk for a moment about his human owner, a dog-show judge and boxer breeder from Iowa. She has a dream burning in her soul, a dream of building the most perfect boxer ever.

She begins with the ideal mother, her champion show dog, Red Rock's Savored Sweetsong. Then she scours the globe for a sire, the perfect genetic match to create a utopia of paragon boxers.

Oh, the thrill of discovery when she finds him! Even his name brings a chill: Champion Sullisbury's Starry Fire.

But there's one teensy problem. He lives half a world away.

What now? Give up?

No. Medical advancements save the day. Champion Sullisbury's Starry Fire's semen arrives via airmail. Expensive? Oh yeah. But worth every penny.

The breeder watches over her pregnant prize. She dotes. She pampers. The day comes for X-rays. How many pups nestle and jostle within the womb of Red Rock's Savored Sweetsong?

Two.

All that effort, all that expense for so few pups? This calls for a recalculation of her cost:benefit ratio.

Still worth it. Barely.

Then again, for the love of the breed, for the chance to create perfection, is any price too great?

Delivery day arrives. The first pup glows shiny white all over.

Oops.

White boxers don't meet breed standard. White boxers can't be bred, shown, studded. White boxers are nice pets, not sculpted perfection.

Defeat crushes the breeder's chest. Fifty percent of her investment is white. What if the other pup follows suit?

She waits. She watches. She frets.

She waits some more.

The next pup squeezes its way into the world. Rich brown fur covers his back and sides. A flawless white horseshoe mark adorns his luscious black mask. Exquisite white stocking feet. Gorgeous lines. Stunning head. Luxuriously long legs.

Perfect.

The breeder's formerly crushed chest pops with pride. She calls him Cash—aka Worth Every Penny.

Days go by. The pup's eyes open. He grows strong and frisky. The breeder's friends come bearing compliments for the exquisitely proportioned, quintessentially marked puppy. He has everything.

Er, except testicles.

Well, he has one, and presumably another on the way. But time scurries by, and no second testicle drops into position.

A flaw. An eliminator.

A nice pet.

End of show career.

❖

My hubby, Alan, and I don't have a pooch in our plans. I'm homeschooling our two boys, we're involved in church activities, and then our sons join a traveling soccer team, meaning every Saturday Alan and I drive very far, sit in foul weather, and watch twenty-two children stampede after an evasive ball. Our lives feel like a never-ending Tilt-O-Whirl ride. The last thing we need is a pet.

But doggie longing hits our youngest son especially hard. What do you do when your kid keeps knocking at your neighbors' door, asking if their dog can come out to play?

We do what any normal parents would do—we move out of the state.

Across the country, to be exact.

Okay, it's not really because of our son. Alan takes a different job. While it's a terrific opportunity for him, our boys are less enthusiastic. We tear them away from the place they were born, the house where they fingerprinted every wall and even some ceilings, the swing set they jumped off of, the yard where they played baseball, and the trees they climbed. We make them say good-bye to their church, their friends, and the bedroom we painted with red, blue, and white racing stripes.

Oh, the guilt.

Oh, the soul searching.

Oh, the bribery.

Enter Henry.

One testicle short of the show-dog ring, Henry ought to have all the right qualities of a family dog—playful (for two energetic boys), loving (because boxers are known for being people oriented), and a promising guard-dog physique (for the hulking appearance of a protector).

I drive hours to pick him up, but I don't mind. What better salve to soothe the boys' lonesome hearts than a warm puppy?

The most reasonable plan always has a flaw.

Does anyone else think it's a bad sign when, on your puppy's first visit to PetSmart, flabbergasted bystanders mention the words *obedience school*?

Alan and I are all aquiver to take Henry to the pet store. When you have a cute puppy, you want to show him off. His gorgeous lines and born-to-be-a-show-dog prance make people smile and nudge one another, pointing as Henry passes by. No lie.

We round the corner into the kibble aisle, and a horse-size dog blocks the entire Purina selection. Henry bursts ahead to meet him. Maybe *meet* is the wrong word. More like *challenge*—head up, tail up, with a ramrod-straight back and a bad attitude.

How did my cutesy puppy turn into an evil Chuck Norris?

The other dog—apparently an Irish wolfhound/Clydesdale cross—behaves like a gentleman. He stretches down his mighty neck and gives Henry a look that says, "Do you get that my head is bigger than your whole body?"

Nope. Itty-bitty nose to whoppin' huge nose, Henry overlooks the glaringly obvious.

The wolfhound's jaws—large enough to swallow Henry whole—open.

I suck in a breath, but Henry doesn't flinch.

The wolfhound merely yawns in one massive sigh, then gives his owners a look that says, "You see what I have to put up with? Why do you bring me here?"

The wolfhound's owners, however, turn to us.

"Has he always been that way?" The man's voice has that quiet tone reserved for fatal diseases.

I look at my darling puppy. "What way?"

"You know, showing dominance to other dogs?"

There's some tact for you, because he neglects to mention Henry's sheer idiocy for staring down a dog that outweighs him by a hundred pounds.

"I don't know. This is the first time we've seen him interact with another dog." Perhaps that was a puppy purchase boo-boo?

"Oh." The man's gaze roves over Henry and then back to me. "He's a pretty dog. Where did you get him?"

"From a woman in Iowa."

"Didn't she say anything about his temperament?"

"Now that you mention it, I think she told me he and his sibling used to tussle for dominance . . . a lot."

A knowing look passes between the couple. The man runs his hand down the wolfhound's gray flank. "Dominance issues can lead to trouble. Didn't she say anything about obedience classes?"

"I guess she did bring that up. We'll get to it at some point."

"We went to K9 University over on Northwest Expressway. Can't recommend them highly enough. They have puppy classes." He takes another look at iron-back Henry. "I'd start now."

Alan and I blink at each other. I suddenly know what it feels like to go to the school open house and learn you have the problem child. What's a parent to do?

Denial. Always a good first choice.

We try that approach for a week or two, as more problems trickle to the surface, like little disaster dog's fascination—make that cling-till-death obsession—for all things flapping. I relive some form of this conversation every time I enter a room:

"Hey, Alan, have you seen—Arrrgghhh! Henry, no! Let go of my pants!"

Grrrrrrrrrrrrrrr chomp chomp tug tug tug

"NO, Henry!"

Grrrrr tug tug rriiiiiiipppppp

Perhaps I should have listened more closely when the breeder said Henry liked to tug at her jeans. Somehow that didn't translate to "mangle."

Henry meets our every "no" with a "Yeah, right. Make me." It's not that we don't try to find creative ways to discipline him. How hard can it be? We read the books. Surely we outrank him in IQ.

Except, for a dog who lacks the sense to recognize a wolfhound's inherent bigness, he quickly discovers we can't discipline him if we can't catch him. Thus is born the game Ring Around the Coffee Table.

I know we're in trouble the first time he swipes a pencil. We chase our dodging doggie all through the house before I realize his thrill is in the pursuit.

I jerk to a halt. Henry skids to a stop on the other side of the coffee table.

I shoot him an I-mean-business glare. "Drop it."

His eyes dance.

"I'm not going to chase you anymore. You can't make me. Put the pencil down."

Crunch.

Rats. How dangerous will that be in his stomach?

Crunch, crunch.

"You're a stinker, Henry."

His ears perk in a "Yippee, you're gonna play with me!" look.

Why couldn't we get a dog who moves at sloth speed? It takes two people to corner him, and by that time he's completely forgotten the crime. Plus he wriggles with glee.

Ever try correcting a happy puppy? It's like telling a toddler to throw away the big frosted cookie you just gave him.

Aside from discipline problems, our cute little bundle of trouble has another issue: zero bladder control.

What freak of nature makes fluid output ten times greater than fluid input?

"Just pour a little vinegar right on the puddle, and soak it up with paper towels," the breeder had said. "Then he won't smell his excrement and think that's his toilet area."

Works like a charm. He never pees in the same place twice. Not really a help when you think about it. Why didn't the breeder tell me I'd need enough vinegar to pickle the state of Ohio?

But here's the kicker: the mad pottier still manages to bamboozle us with puppy charm. This is God's clever design so that when Henry is evil we don't wring his fuzzy little neck. It's not long before I notice a corollary. The higher the cuteness factor, the more devious the dog.

Useful tip for potential dog owners: get an ugly dog.

3

Henry's next issue is the most worrisome yet: random bursts of hazardous intelligence. He swiftly pinpoints which child in the family is, um, attention-challenged, and targets him for a little game called Stalk the Kid's Food. If my son wanders two steps from his half-eaten hot dog, it's good-bye, Oscar Mayer.

The trouble is, not all people-food, and definitely not all people-toys, are safe for doggie ingestion. Combine brilliance and stubbornness with a total lack of common sense, and you have disaster. The time has come for professional help.

We call K9 University and sign up for classes. They aren't free, by the way. Nothing is free when it comes to owning a dog. If anyone ever tries to give you a dog for free, run. Very fast. You are on your way to being royally had.

Week one of dog discipline gives instruction on how to keep your pooch from walking *you*. Picture a large room filled with puppies and their owners going in mostly opposite directions. We fit right in.

Except at quiet listening time.

I'm riveted to the instructor's lecture, trying to maximize every dollar of the course fee we've paid, and Henry's about as placid as a demolition derby.

He wants to tug on the leash. Or ambush someone's pants. Or bark raucously at the benign poodle licking its rear end next to us.

One of the first lessons on the instructor's agenda? How to Break Up a Dogfight 101. I hope that's standard and not because of Henry's misbehavior.

Week two's agenda is Sit. Amazingly, many dogs do, in fact, sit. Even Henry. I think he's merely lulling us into a false sense of security.

Next week they teach the Lie Down session.

Total catastrophe. Well, for us. Everyone else's dog gets it figured out. It's not a hard concept when you're wearing a choke collar. You lie down, you get to breathe.

Not Henry.

I pull down on his collar. He plants his feet and thrusts his jaw in the air.

The collar tightens. He resists.

I continue firm downward pressure just like the instructor says. Henry's eyeballs bulge.

He starts wriggling, then coughing. In seconds, he ratchets the trauma to a gasping choke. Pretty soon the whole crowd can't miss his horrible hucking-up-a-lung noise.

Nothing like having your own melodrama in front of a class of calm, recumbent dogs.

"Come on, Henry." My self-conscious glance darts around the room. *"Platz."*

Platz is the word we'll use for "down." At K9 University, they give the option of teaching you German-based commands in case you want to have your dog trained in personal protection. That way your dog responds to words a potential attacker won't know. Theoretically.

We have delusions that Henry might go through that training someday, except I'm pretty sure failing puppy class will disqualify him.

Downward pressure. "You can do it, Henry. Platz."

Aaaack, aack, gasp, whine.

Good grief, could this kill him? I picture being the first person at obedience class to accidentally murder her dog. That'll probably disqualify him from personal protection class too.

Surely he'll give in before it comes to that? It's just a question of who's more stubborn.

I pour on the pressure, which requires ridiculous contortions that never actually produce better leverage.

Alan and I take turns with the circus act, and even our boys give it a shot. Just when we think we've nearly got the dog plastered to the ground, he squirts away like a four-legged Houdini.

Yippee. We get to start all over with the choke-and-gag routine. At times it degrades into full-body wrestling. This is not what you picture when you think of obedience class.

The instructor takes pity on us. "Henry doesn't seem to want to lie down. Would you like me to try?"

I hand the leash to her and step back. Henry gulps a deep breath and prepares for round seventy-two.

She loops the leather once around her wrist. "The trick is to be firm. He needs to know you're in charge."

Probably a concept he's missing in our case. We're only in charge when he doesn't want to be.

Which is never.

"Platz." She uses a perfect German accent and perfect down-ward pressure.

Henry braces for the long haul.

She applies more pressure.

Henry grits his teeth and makes like a statue.

I suppose this isn't nice, but I'm strangely comforted by the fact that he won't listen to her either.

She pulls harder. "Well, he's certainly a bit stubborn about it."

Rigor mortis has nothing on that dog's locked legs.

I glance at the floor. "Maybe he doesn't like the cold concrete."

She kneels over him. "He still has to do what you tell him to do. Like it or not."

More pressure.

Henry the gangly puppy—he weighs all of twenty-three pounds—prevails.

The instructor sets her jaw and performs her own set of contortions. Somehow she still manages to look dignified.

Aaaack, aack, choke, whine . . . sigh.

What's that? Do my ears detect a crack in Henry's iron will?

The poor instructor is practically lying on the floor now, and Henry sees fit to drop a whole half inch. Then another. And another.

She has him.

His belly brushes concrete.

With all the grace of a centipede on ice skates, Henry claws at the floor. Then he pops up like a deranged jack-in-the-box.

Nevertheless, the instructor had won. Henry had, in fact, lain. Albeit momentarily.

She passes the leash to me. "You're going to need to practice that at home. A lot."

Big news.

Is the dog hideously stubborn, or does he just have a mortal fear of concrete? It's cold, I'll admit that. And he doesn't have much belly fur.

How would I feel if my bare tummy hit that floor?

Maybe Henry deserves a little consideration. A deal of sorts. We won't make him lie down in class if, for pity's sake, the dog will at least try to obey on carpeting.

Except, under the guise of being reasonable, I'm bargaining with my dog—a half-wit toddler incapable of rational thought.

What does that make me?

One of the great things about obedience class is the question-and-answer period. Not that Henry always cooperates with listening time—he wants to play when he wants to play.

Period.

In between Henry's embarrassing outbursts, we learn a lot.

The instructor looks over our class. "Okay, any issues this week?"

I raise my hand. "Um, we can't seem to get Henry to understand that urinating is for outside . . ."

"Limit the size of his play area. That will help. When it gets too big, it's easy for him to sneak off to do his business."

Yes, we definitely have a stealth pee-er on our hands.

"Also," she continues, "take him out the same way every time so he gets in the habit of going to that door. Eventually he'll connect it with potty time. Don't forget to go regularly and praise him whenever he piddles outside."

The next week I raise my hand again. "We've been trying all the recommendations for the peeing issue, but it doesn't seem to be working."

"How old is Henry?"

"About three and a half months."

"You've seen no improvement whatsoever?"

I look at Alan. "Well, maybe just the slightest bit."

Alan nods.

"Be consistent. I know it's frustrating, but he'll get it. Just like with kids. None of them ever wear diapers to kindergarten."

That's a sore subject. My boys took forever to potty train. We made it before kindergarten, but preschool? Not so much. What law of probability did we have to break to go three-for-three in toity-training late bloomers?

At the start of the third week's question-and-answer time, my hand, as usual, shoots into the air.

"Henry keeps biting the bark off a tree in our yard."

The instructor leans forward like maybe she didn't hear us right. "He's biting a tree?"

"Yeah."

"Every tree?"

"Just the one. I don't know why." I scan the faces of my classmates. Don't their dogs do weird things?

Apparently not.

"The thing is, it's not our tree. We're renting the house. I don't want to be responsible for killing someone's hickory. It's like fifty years old."

The instructor's forehead crinkles. "How 'bout distracting him with his favorite toy?"

"I think the tree *is* his favorite toy. We can get him to do other things, but he always goes back to the tree. It's like a giant Nylabone calling his name."

"You've tried correcting him?"

"Yeah. But it's a bummer to make him wear his leash all the time in the yard. Is there anything else we can try?"

An encouraging smile fans across her face. "Sure. You can get some Bitter Apple spray. We sell it in our store area, or you can try a local pet shop."

"Bitter Apple spray?"

"Smells bad, tastes bad. A definite discouragement. Just spray it on the tree."

My eyebrows hitch up. "Would that work on his leash also? Sometimes when we walk him he manages to snatch it with his teeth. Then he tries to pull it from us."

Nothing like walking your puppy while he's facing you, playing tug-of-war. Must every outing leave a wake of chuckling spectators?

"You'd better spray his leash too."

I turn to Alan and whisper, "We're not leavin' without that stuff."

"Got that right," Alan whispers back.

We both shoot Henry a look.

He flashes us his "happy puppy" face, complete with perky ears, head slightly cocked, and big, dopey eyes. What instinct parks his features like that every time we have to shell out the dough?

After class we scoot to the store area. A man leans against the counter. "Can I help you find something?"

The door next to him opens, and our instructor walks in. "Oh, have you met Angel yet? He's the owner of K9 University."

Angel gives us both a hearty handshake, then turns his attention to our puppy, who's prancing around on high cute-alert. "Who's this?"

"That's Henry." I'm all puffed with cute-puppy ownership.

Angel comes around the counter. "Hi, Henry. How're ya doin', guy? Are you a good boy?"

Henry's body curves into jelly, and he wiggles his way to Angel. Instant love.

"Aw." Angel somehow knows exactly where Henry most likes to be petted. "What a good boy. Yeah, I'll pet you . . ."

I watch as Henry shamelessly fawns over Angel. Isn't this supposed to be *our* dog? I think he's ready to abandon us forever. "I guess he likes you."

Angel chuckles. "He just loves attention. Don't you, Henry?"

Henry wriggles and jiggles in sheer delight.

Then he pees on the man.

My eyes shoot wide open. That didn't really happen?

Dark stains lace across Angel's pants and shoes, and a puddle spreads on the floor.

Heat flushes my face. "I'm so sorry!"

Can you get kicked out of puppy school for peeing on the principal?

Angel laughs. "He got me, all right." Then he gives Henry another pat. "Yup, you got me."

How do you like that? My fawning puppy leaves his mark, and Angel rolls right along. I knew we'd like this place. After all, they helped train a giant Irish wolfhound not to snack on troublemaking puppies.

The instructor grabs a mop and makes quick work of the puddle. Obviously, they've had accidents before, so I feel a little better.

Well no, I don't, but I try to think I do.

We buy our Bitter Apple spray and hightail it out of there before Henry can tinkle on something else.

The next week, we actually show our faces again.

The instructor smiles at the class. "So, any questions or concerns this week?"

Up goes my hand.

Bless that instructor's heart, she doesn't even look annoyed.

"We tried the Bitter Apple spray, but it doesn't seem to be working. I mean, it worked at first, but then Henry lost his aversion to it."

"Well, it does wear off. Did you try spraying again?"

"Yep. It helped most when it was freshly sprayed. We've gone through half a bottle already. But now I think he likes it."

She eyes Henry. "Well, a small percentage of dogs don't seem negatively affected by Bitter Apple. Henry must be one of those."

Of course. Because we can't get a normal dog that does normal stuff. Why, God, did we have to get a dog-anomaly?

"I can give you a recipe for pepper spray," the instructor says. "You can make it yourself with red pepper and vinegar. Most dogs respond to that if Bitter Apple doesn't work."

Most dogs? I don't hold out much hope. But there's good news. We'll be moving to a new house soon, and all the trees will be outside our fenced yard.

As we leave that day, we stop at the counter of the store to get the pepper spray recipe.

"Henn-ryyy." Angel says it like his day isn't complete without a glimpse of the little guy.

Henry spots his best pal and shakes with glee.

Angel gives him a rubdown. "How're ya doin', Henry?"

My puppy answers with a wriggle, wriggle, fawn, fawn, PEE.

"Oh, my gosh. I'm so sorry."

Angel chuckles. "No problem. That's why I wear boots to work."

So this happens regularly? My guess is yes. I mean, if Angel has Henry—one of the world's most stubbornly dominant dogs—piddling in submission, what about all the nice dogs? How many times a day does this poor man get tinkled on?

Angel seems to have that intangible something. And I don't mean fire hydrant fragrance. Dogs respect him. No wonder he teaches the advanced obedience classes—he knows what he's doing. Oh, to soak up some of that wisdom. He trains drug sniffing dogs and search and rescue dogs and all that cool stuff. Boy, if I could get Henry into—

My eyes sweep over Henry's latest puddle. Are we even going to pass puppy class? The dog needs serious remedial help. Our instructor says training takes time, but it already seems like Henry's getting more attention than my kids. What have I gotten myself into?

I understand puppies come with a certain amount of inconvenience, but I pictured it more like a fender bender. Henry's starting to look like a world-class pileup. Would my childhood dog have been this way if we'd have gotten him as a puppy? Is it only a matter of holding out through the early trials, and then the rewards come down the road?

Why does the road look really, really long?

4

Remember the days of Travel with Babies? This is a game where you collect your kiddies, gather the requisite baby paraphernalia (i.e., all of it), cram your car just shy of exploding, and then pray your little darlings don't have barfing bouts, diaper blowouts, or trapped-in-a-car-seat tantrums all the way to your destination.

We've never had the luxury of living close to extended family, so we've played—and survived—this delightful activity many a time. At Christmas, our grandparent tours always include a weeklong visit. A dog never figured into the equation. Once Henry arrives, a disturbing question arises. How can we fit four people, boots, coats, suitcases, a dog with all his doggie stuff, *and* Christmas presents for the entire family into one minivan?

We consider staying home, but we've just moved to Oklahoma, and we're temporarily living in a rented house. Most of our possessions, Christmas decorations included, are still packed, so it doesn't feel like Christmas for the boys. We need that road trip. But we can't leave Henry home, duct taped to the couch with the remote control in his paw. We'll have to find a place to board him. That doesn't sound too hard.

Ha.

The first place I call wants twenty bucks a day. The next place doesn't have room. Neither does the third. The fourth place wants thirty bucks a day. Yikes!

"That seems a little steep," I tell the gal on the phone.

"Well, it includes one play session out in the yard."

"Play session?"

"You know, time for the dog to get out of his crate and run around."

"He's going to be in a crate all day?" How did this reality escape me?

"He'll be let out twice a day to relieve himse—"

"Twice a day? He's a puppy. He potties about eighty-five times a day."

"Well, he can urinate in his crate if he has to."

That's the way to work on the ol' potty training.

"You can pay for more play sessions if you're worried about it."

"Pay for play sessions?"

"It's ten dollars per twenty-minute personal play session."

"Ten dollars?"

Her voice takes on a clipped tone. "It's a *personal* session. Someone here will interact and play with him."

My spine bristles. I have to pay those people to interact with my cuddly dog? Isn't there a universal desire to frolic with cute puppies—at least among people who choose to work for a boarding kennel? Clearly, I'm naïve in the ways of puppy big business.

"I think I'll do some more checking around."

"We're filling up fast."

Okay, we're new in town. Are people in Oklahoma desperate? Or do they just have more money than we do? Or maybe they're smart enough to book all the good places well in advance, and Paying-for-Play Kennel is all that's left.

Perhaps my first mistake was browsing the phone book. We know a few people in town who have dogs. Where do they board them?

Nowhere, as it turns out.

They all have teensy dogs that travel in teensy crates and require nothing but teensy toys and a teensy bag of dog food.

Perhaps my second mistake was getting a big dog.

Hours later, the glaringly obvious answer arrives in my frontal lobe. K9 University. Surely they can recommend a good kennel. I find their number and punch it into my phone.

When the gal answers, I tell her we attended their classes, and ask if she knows a reliable kennel where we could board our dog.

"We do boarding here. What kind of dog do you have?"

My body snaps upright. "We have a four-month-old boxer named Henry."

"Oh, Henry! How's he doing?"

She remembers him? Then again, he likes the taste of Bitter Apple spray, has a tree-biting fetish, doesn't sit quietly during instruction, and tinkles on the owner. How could she forget him?

Amazingly, she still seems to like him. He did graduate from the puppy obedience class. Barely.

"I think he's getting better. But he sometimes still piddles in the house and chews on our pant legs. And pulls bark off the tree. And nips at us. And jumps on us . . ."

She laughs. "Don't forget he's still a puppy. Keep doing his training every day. It's going to take time and persistence. When he's five months old, you can always sign him up for our next class."

"Oh, we'll be there, or Henry will take over the house."

She laughs again.

"Tell me about the boarding. Does he have to stay in a crate all day?"

"You remember those big caged areas that line the side of the classroom arena? That's where the dogs stay. We move the dogs out during class time so they won't disrupt it."

Seriously? No crating? A caged area to himself? Room to walk, play a bit, and more important, urinate somewhere that isn't his crate? What's not to love?

"Can we bring his crate to keep in there with him? He's used to sleeping in it at night."

"Of course. There's plenty of room. We want him to be comfortable."

These people are too good to be true. There has to be a catch. "Um, what's the price?"

"Let me check."

I hold my breath.

She clackety-clacks on a keyboard for a moment, then gives me a price.

My eyebrows about shoot off my head. How can they be making any money? "That's extremely reasonable."

"We give our clients a discount. We know the dogs, and they've had some training. That makes it easier on us."

Right. But you know what it really is? They love dogs there. Even Henry.

"Oh, we'll also reinforce his training when we take him outside every day."

"Wow, that's terrific. Thanks!"

"He's doing German commands, right?"

"Yeah. But you probably ought to skip 'platz' when you're on the concrete . . ."

"Right."

My whole body goes weightless. I didn't realize until that moment what it would mean to find a trustworthy kennel for Henry. Sort of like when we'd found those college student gems over the years who loved kids and happily babysat our boys.

But our boys never caused the kind of nuisance for their sitters Henry did at K9 University. Still, they're professionals. If anyone can keep Henry out of trouble, they can.

The first thing Angel tells me when I come to pick up Henry after Christmas is how much everyone enjoyed having him there. I have to wonder if we're talking about the same dog.

Angel grins. "Remember that old TV show *Cheers*? Whenever Norm came into the bar, the whole crowd shouted, 'Norm!' It's like that with Henry. I don't know why, but every time we see him, we go, 'Henn-ryyy!'"

I'm now certain there's such a thing as doggie charisma.

"So, I guess he had a good time here."

"Yeah. He's a riot. Sometimes when I came in to do paperwork, I'd let him hang out in my office with me. You should've seen him show off when I opened his kennel door. He stuck his nose in the air and skipped in front of the other dogs, like, 'Ha ha, I'm out and you're not.' What a goof."

"You let him in your office?" As in, you like him enough that I don't have to pay you extra to play with him?

"Sure."

I can't help but glance at the man's pant cuffs. But really, what am I thinking? Like Henry would dare lay a tooth on this paragon of pack leaders?

"So he was good, then?"

"Mostly."

Uh-oh.

Angel gives Henry a pet. "He did escape one night."

My eyes go wide.

"Oh, he's fine, don't worry. But he caused a bit of mischief here . . ."

A bit of mischief? Right. Angel's an easygoing guy. A bit of mischief could mean Henry shredded their tax returns or something.

A half grin edges up Angel's cheek. "Yeah, I got this phone call from the police at 3:00 a.m."

Oh, dear. The police are involved?

"They said my alarm got tripped. I asked if it was from inside or outside. When they said inside, I knew no one had broken in. I figured a dog escaped and was wandering around the classroom arena. I told them I'd handle it myself."

Okay, breathe. No police.

Angel leans casually against the store counter. "I didn't worry too much. I got out of bed and drove over here. But when I pulled up to the building and my headlights shone into the glass doors of the store area, I knew I was in trouble."

When he says "trouble," I somehow know "Henry" will be the next word out of his mouth.

"Henry stood at the doors."

"The doors? Of the store?"

"Somehow he made it out of his kennel, out of the training arena, and broke into the store area."

"I wonder if he was scared. I mean, he's just a little guy." I swallow past a lump of pity that suddenly rises in my throat.

"I don't think that was a problem for him."

Oh, right. This is Henry we're talking about. What would a deviant like Henry do all alone in the middle of the night at this great big school? Find the toys and celebrate Christmas in his own special way.

"He recognized me at the door, and his whole body started wriggling and wagging like I was his best friend." He pauses for a grin, then continues. "The store was trashed."

Trashed? Dollar signs flash before my eyes.

Angel chuckles. "He pulled every single thing he could reach off the wall. Chewed it, ate it, played with it, mangled it. *Everything*. All over the floor. Literally."

My shoulders sag. Henry, faced with the mother of all doggie fantasies, couldn't just pick a few toys, a few treats, maybe a Bitter

Apple spray or two. No. My dog had to destroy the store's entire inventory from waist-level down.

Angel shakes his head. "I wanted to be mad, but he was just so proud of himself, prancing around and wiggling. How do you stay mad at a happy puppy?"

Yeah. Welcome to my world.

I glare at my naughty pooch.

Henry, bright eyed and quivering with enthusiasm, gazes back with a face that says, "Are we gonna play now? Huh? Huh? Can we? Huh?"

Right.

"Angel, I'm so sorry. What do we owe you for that?"

And can we have a payment plan?

He shrugs a shoulder. "Nothin'. It's the cost of doing business."

My mouth drops open. "A-are you sure? I mean, it was our dog."

"Don't worry about it. Really."

I don't even know how to begin to argue, or whether I should, so I simply thank him. Profusely. And thank God for the gift of nice people.

Nicer still, these people willingly board Henry again and again. They don't even charge us extra for hazardous duty. I can't help but wonder if they've got a special Henry-proof kennel now, with three computer-controlled locks and a redundant system of laser sensors that seal off the store area, just in case.

Even with our experiences in obedience class, I don't think I grasp just how different Henry is from ordinary dogs until I send an email to a friend, saying, "Alan's taken Jacob and Jonathan to baseball practice. Even better, he took the dog. I'm alone in the house. Yippee!"

She writes back, "You can't be alone when the dog is there? Is he that much like a person?"

"He's worse. He's a menace." You can never feel alone—or even find three seconds of peace—while Henry roams the house.

Not that we despise him or anything. He has a weirdly endearing charisma that surely comes from his show-dog genes. Everywhere we go, Henry makes sure people notice him. We can't even have a basic, ordinary walk. Oh, we take him, but Henry doesn't walk. He prances. Ears cocked, nose in the air, his paws springing along the turf like happiness itself. This dog was born to be ogled. There's a certain amount of fun to owning a pet like that, even if he does come with a difficult side. But fun and love are two different things.

One day I drive the boys and their friend home from a baseball game. The kids lounge in the back of the van, chatting baseball, superheroes, and who knows what. They snag my attention when they start discussing what time it is. They have a good reason to care.

"I think it's after five," Jonathan says.

Jacob crosses his arms. "Well then, I hope it takes a long time to get home."

"I don't!"

"What, you've got something to do?" their friend says.

Jacob turns to him. "No. If it's after five, then it's my Henry-turn."

"Henry-turn?"

Jonathan blows out a long sigh. "We have to take turns watching our dog."

"Following him around so he doesn't get in all our stuff. Jonathan has even hours, and I have odd."

I catch the boy's knitted brow in the rearview mirror.

"I have a dog, and I don't have to do that."

"Well, Henry's still a puppy," Jacob says.

The boy's frown deepens. "Our dog was a puppy when we got him, and I don't remember—"

"Our dog needs constant supervision." Jacob rolls his eyes.

"Otherwise he eats stuff," Jonathan says.

"Like pencils and pens."

"He already chewed up three Nintendo controllers—"

"The TV remote—"

"No, *two* remotes—"

"Brio train tracks—"

"A car from my racetrack set—"

"Legos—"

"Baseballs—"

"Tupperware—"

Their friend's head swivels back and forth while Jacob and Jonathan recite the litany of casualties. Finally he interrupts. "Your dog sounds like a lot of trouble. I didn't think they . . . wow . . . I'm glad my dog is . . . normal."

An anvil of guilt lodges in my gut. This, the one and only dog experience my kids will have, isn't much of a treat. The boys aren't exaggerating Henry's behavior one bit. He does require constant vigilance. And it's not like we don't exercise him, or don't give him toys to play with or constructive things to chew. He just wants our stuff instead. Or wants to cause trouble. Or feels the unquenchable need to live like a rogue torpedo.

He doesn't even seem to be bonding with us. Maybe because he never sits still long enough. We spend our days trailing him from one disaster to another, and if our attention lapses, I find myself making a ridiculous phone call to the veterinarian. Take the soap incident, for example.

"Meadows Veterinary Clinic. How may I help you?"

"My dog ate a bar of soap!"

"Soap?" The woman's voice holds a ring of disbelief.

"Mickey Mouse soap from Disney World." Why we still have

several bars of the stuff months and months after vacation when my boys are supposed to wash with it daily is beside the point.

She doesn't laugh, but she still sounds dubious. "Did he lick it or genuinely bite it?"

"He *ate* it! The whole bar. What should I do?"

"Does he look sick?"

I peer at Henry. He's got a jaunty "What shall we do next?" tip to his head. "Well no, actually. He looks just fine."

"He ate the whole bar?"

"Yes. I don't know why."

"It'll probably just pass through his system. If he's not uncomfortable, I wouldn't worry about it."

"Oh. Okay. Thanks . . ."

Fortunately I don't have to give my name. Come to think of it, I neglect to identify myself on the next call as well.

"Meadows Veterinary Clinic. How may I help you?"

I trail Henry in a circuit around the kitchen, dining room, and hallway to keep my gaze riveted to him. "My dog swallowed a chicken leg, bone and all. Will that be dangerous?"

"How much did he chew it?"

"No chewing. Snatched. Swallowed. Gone in one and a half seconds."

"Is he in pain?"

I kick into double-time to keep up with Henry. "Pain? No, I guess not."

"What's he doing?"

"Running around. Probably looking for more chicken."

"Well, it should work through his system."

I keep on hearing that phrase. I ought to stamp it across the dog's head.

The next emergency call I make will go something like this:

"Hi, Meadows Veterinary Clinic? This time Henry . . . um . . . never mind. I'm sure he'll survive."

And he always does. But could someone tell me why any dog in his right mind would pull tissues out of a box and consume them one by one? Do they taste better than his dog food? I feel silly having to place Kleenex out of the dog's reach. Worse, he's just as happy to dig used tissues out of the wastebasket. You blow your nose at our house, and you have to seal away the evidence like hazardous waste.

Napkins sit in an attractive holder on the kitchen table until we discover mysterious scratches running along the tabletop. Yep. Henry. For no mentally stable reason, he hikes himself up, plants his paws on the table, and then swipes at the napkin holder with his nice long nails.

The table needs refinishing now. As does every door in the house. Boxers are paw-ers. Cute when they're playfully cuffing toys. Not so cute when they're trying to claw through a door.

And while I'm mentioning damage, where can we buy new window screens? It's not enough for him to tear the mesh. When the windows are open, he has to bounce against the screens and mangle their frames into unrecognizable pieces of aluminum. That'll be fun to explain at the repair store.

Does my life have some sort of pandemonium shortage that God means to cure by plaguing me with this creature? I mean, how else can I explain an anomaly like Henry? I'll admit longing for the perfect boxer of my childhood. But what I have here is the canine embodiment of the Tasmanian devil.

5

Henry's five-month birthday present is more obedience classes. Our sons think it's a rotten gift on par with a box of dress clothes, but Henry's thrilled. Not about the obedience part; about going to K9 University. He loves it there.

With Henry's puppy physique maturing into muscle, it doesn't take long for the instructors to recommend a pinch collar. "It helps control strong dogs who ignore regular choke collars."

Henry? Disregard a choke collar? Whatever gave them that idea?

We buy one that day. It comes with steel prongs that dig into Henry's neck when we apply a firm yank. Don't get me wrong—the prongs aren't sharp. They simply simulate the feel of a mother dog biting around a puppy's neck to discipline her little miscreant.

Provided we do it right. Which we don't.

In our defense, it's a complicated contraption requiring much instruction just to put the thing on. Once we master that, the art of the tug comes next.

"It's a sharp jerk and release," Angel says. "You're not trying to strangle him. You're trying to get his attention and break off his behavior."

It sounds easy.

Therefore, we have trouble.

We don't really want to hurt him, so we tug too gently. Ever have your kid laugh at you when you spank him? This is the dog equivalent.

Angel performs a precision pulling gesture in the air. "You have to give it a good hard yank."

We try that next, but we tug with too small a motion and release too quickly. Consequently, we merely rake in the slack and let it go. No pinch. But hey, we have the "near-discipline" maneuver mastered. If you want to almost correct your dog, we can help you.

On my next attempt, Henry jumps up on me, and while I fumble with the leash—I'm going to give a good hard yank this time—he plunks his feet down and turns toward Alan. That's when my strangling pull hits him.

He whirls around with a look of shock, then I see the wheels in his mind turning: *Hmm, jump on the lady—good. Welcome the balding guy—painful.*

Not too soft, not too small, not too slow. I didn't know coordination was a requirement for dog ownership. Shouldn't there be warnings? Maybe something like:

Caution: Do not purchase unless you possess the reflexes of a fighter pilot, the fine motor skills of a neurosurgeon, the dexterity of Michael Jordan, and a black belt in karate. Nobel Prize in physics optional.

The good news? Henry provides plenty of opportunity for practice, so we do improve over time. Sort of. But how do you know the exact moment he's going to do something bad so you're ready with your expert yank?

I ask Angel about this one day.

He smiles. "You set him up."

"Huh?"

"Well, say you want to correct his jumping behavior. You get the leash on him and put him in a situation where he'll want to jump. You let him do it, then give the correction."

I make him want to be bad, then punish him for being bad? That just sounds evil.

We do it anyway.

Except Henry doesn't want to be bad when we're ready for it. We manage a few inept corrections, but not enough to make a difference. When we take the leash off, he's more than happy to be bad.

Caution: Do not purchase unless you possess the patience of Mother Teresa. And Job. And Nelson Mandela.

Next we try leaving the leash on all the time.

"Just make sure you always supervise him," Angel tells us. "The leash can get caught on something and hurt the dog."

Good to know.

But guess what? When you're trailing a leash, it catches on everything. The poor dog walks around getting random yanks from table legs, doors, chairs, you name it. Heaven help him if he rolls on the ground. Four legs and a leash become a spaghetti mess in five seconds flat.

He tries to kick his legs free, but instead jerks the leash in a perfect discipline tug—the kind I'm still incapable of. Except Henry doesn't know what he's in trouble for, and he doesn't know he's the one yanking, so he keeps on kicking. We have to jump into the fray of flailing legs and try to untangle him faster than he can re-tangle himself.

This has to stop. Back to K9 University for a new plan.

They have one, of course. There's a little handle you can buy to attach to the collar. Then the dog doesn't trail the leash, but you still have something to yank for discipline.

Caution: The purchase of a pet may require accessory purchases. Lots of them. Things you never heard of. You're probably going to get downright grumpy about it. Deal with it.

The little handle has its advantages. No more tangles. No more catching on doors. No more random yanks from table legs. The downside? Try to grab hold of the thing when he's jumping or playing nippy dog.

Still, any help is better than none.

Until the day we get a little lax with our supervision.

We ought to realize something isn't right. It's quiet. Too quiet. And Henry has disappeared.

Then we hear something.

That's always a bad sign. I mean, watch any suspense movie. When the heroine hears a strange sound, it's always something bad. Especially when another character has mysteriously disappeared.

Do we investigate right away? No. We wait until we hear another sound a minute or so later. Something reminiscent of a thud. That's when we get up, dash to the living room, and discover the chair cushion lying in the middle of the floor.

Henry stands nearby, gazing at a nice tear in the cushion.

Did I mention the chair is brand spankin' new? Did I mention that we'd scoured every furniture store within thirty miles for our lovely matching sofa, ottoman, and chair? Did I perhaps mention that the stupid chair alone cost $600?

I thought not.

The cushion sports a nice new hole right on the front. We can't hide it with a flip, and the zipper location doesn't allow for a rotation.

Caution: May ruin furniture. And other stuff. Lots of other stuff. Much more than you are picturing right now. There is no way to prepare for the doggie apocalypse.

The good news is that Henry didn't die of strangulation when his pronged collar stuck in the cushion while we sat idly watching TV in the next room.

But let's ask ourselves, how did he get stuck on the cushion to begin with? I mean, what did he have to do to make that happen? And why would he be doing it?

More random, inexplicable behavior we will never understand.

Until we discover his penchant for cleaning his face on our furniture.

> Caution: Not designed for squeamish sensibilities. May choose furniture, draperies, hanging clothes, or precious heirlooms as napkins. Buy stock in a good steam cleaning company. Your dog will single-handedly triple their yearly sales.

The American Kennel Club's website says boxers are known to desire affection from children and to be patient with them.

I'm not sure Henry got the memo.

He discovers the joy of tugging vines one day while he roams the yard of our rented house. From the open porch window, I see Jacob pull him away from the vines. Henry trots right back to the game.

Again Jacob pulls him away, farther this time, and tries to distract him with another activity. Henry ignores him and goes straight back to the vines. How can a puppy retain that kind of focus? Shouldn't he be like a gnat on caffeine?

Not Henry. I suppose I should consider such single-mindedness astonishing, a sign of mental acuity.

But it's a curse.

Jacob picks up Henry, which I don't normally approve of since he could drop him. But in this case, Jacob does the right disciplinary thing—physical restraint, then removal to another locale.

The moment Henry's body goes airborne, he snaps his puppy jaws at Jacob.

"Henry, no!" Jacob's tone carries more hurt than muscle, and Henry doesn't seem to notice the reproof.

I plow through the door. Granted, the sudden lift probably startled Henry, and his snap fell well shy of Jacob's skin, but I still don't like the behavior. When I reach Henry, he wiggles in joy to see me.

Great. His desperate need to play with the vine sticks in his mind half past forever, but his memory of nipping at my kid slides right off his cortex. How am I supposed to correct him?

On another occasion, Jonathan playfully lumbers to where Henry lies dismantling a squeaky toy. Jonathan spews nonsense patter at him and strokes the fur along Henry's back. Then Jonathan rolls closer, putting his face near the dog's face to give him a kiss.

With a little growl, Henry snaps at Jonathan. The next instant, Henry calmly chews his toy once again.

I gape. Did I really just see that?

Jonathan bursts into tears, I think more from shock than anything. "He bit me!"

I leap up. "No, Henry! No biting."

Startled, Henry jerks his gaze toward me. His look says, "You got a problem with me chewing my toy?"

He doesn't even know why I'm angry?

I can't afford to focus on him when I have an upset kid. "I'm sorry, Jonathan. Henry shouldn't have done that."

"I just wanted to kiss him."

"I know. But Henry thought you were trying to take his toy."

"Dumb dog!"

I hold out my arms. "Come here, sweetie. Let me see your face."

A tiny gash bleeds ever so slightly on Jonathan's cheek. Did Henry really mean to bite him? It seemed more like a doggie disciplinary action—a leave-my-toy-alone statement. Still, we can't have him doing that. Henry should have taken the submissive role and given up the toy.

I email the breeder that day. What if we have a dangerous dog on our hands? Is Henry an anomaly from what the AKC website says, or is this just puppy behavior? Does she see this in her other boxers? And most important, what are we to do about it?

There's a clause in our purchase agreement that requires us to give Henry back to her if for any reason we can no longer take care of him. I understand the spirit of it. She loves her dogs and doesn't want them ending up in a shelter somewhere. Will she feel he's too much of a risk to be placed in a family home? Will she ask for him back?

Then the big question hits me: How would I feel about losing him? About Henry being out of my life?

Right now, not very troubled. He just nipped my kid.

Then I look deeper. With all Henry's cuteness, his charisma, shouldn't I love the dickens out of him? Yet I feel . . . not very attached. Apparently the bond between dog and owner isn't automatic. How did I not know that?

Would it be different if Henry weren't so aloof? It's like his charisma is a show he puts on for the masses, but underneath he's emotionally disengaged.

I compare my feelings to my friend's feelings. She calls one day, her voice shaking, her tone thick with tears. "I've lost Reah . . ."

With the resigned shock of someone who knows she can't change the past and must somehow make do with the future, she unfolds the story of her cat's death. Then weeping overtakes her. The depth of her grief astounds me, the sacredness of a bond forever broken.

I have no words, no comfort that isn't trite. She and I both know only God can mend her gaping wound. All I can do is listen to her, grieve with her, pray for her.

If she's the model of pet owner devotion, I'm not even a ninety-nine cent Mold-A-Rama version. In all fairness, I suppose I wouldn't want a strong attachment right now. I half expect an email from the breeder suggesting we trade dogs, that she'll send us a more compliant, docile specimen that wouldn't dream of nipping a soul.

The days go by. I hear nothing. I figure she's out of town at a dog show.

Two weeks pass. I begin to worry for her. She'd called to see how Henry was doing a couple of weeks after we'd taken him home. During that call, she shared that one of her dogs died of a sudden illness I'd never heard of. Does she have an epidemic over there? Is she neglecting her email because she has too many problems?

A month goes by. Had I sent the email to the right address? I'd gotten it from the breeder's website, which I admit appears long out of date. Had my note gone to some black hole in cyberspace?

All along, I could've simply phoned her. I have her number. I don't know why I don't do it. Denial maybe? Henry can't really be that bad, and he hasn't done it again. We're probably just over-reacting. He's still a puppy.

Or maybe I don't want us to be inept dog owners, incapable of proper discipline.

Maybe we stick it out for the wrong reasons—the ego-stroking fun of owning a charismatic dog everyone seems to notice with oohs and ahhs. No doubt he would've been a smash in the show ring.

Or maybe it's the little whisper. The kind of whisper that's both quiet and loud, that never quite forms into words but somehow nudges a message into your heart.

The whisper that feels like God.

And it feels like we should stay the course.

6

About the time our next road trip rolls around, our travel budget hovers at an all-time low. While I'm hemming and hawing over whether we can afford to board Henry (because who wants to vacation with a tornado), the kennel fills up. End result? Henry gets a ticket on the grandparent tour.

Lousy timing, really. Just when our boys have finally learned to pack for themselves, we take on a permanent toddler who can never be trusted to pack his own things.

"Here, Henry, take this big bag of dog food out to the car for me."

Right. We'll never see him again.

Now I'm stuck packing doggie stuff. I must say, he takes up more than his fair share of space with his crate, his blankies, his food, his dishes, his bones, his treats, his leash, his traveling water bottle, and his shameless pile of toys. Technically, the payload requires a bus, but we shove it all into our minivan and hope we don't blow the tires.

Henry's inaugural vacation is a visit to my parents' house on Lake of the Ozarks—a five-and-a-half-hour trip. Naturally, it takes seven hours. The first stop comes an hour and a half after starting. Bathroom break. Only two occupants have any interest in said break: Alan, because he drinks about a gallon of iced tea every day, and Henry, because, well, the sheer bonanza of unmarked territory is deliriously intoxicating.

Alan slams the car into park at a fast-food restaurant and hops out. Family rules dictate that when one person goes, we all go, so Alan takes the boys with him. That leaves Henry with me.

I snap on his leash and trail him while he tinkles on whatever he can find that needs his mark (which is everything). When he runs dry, I give him a bit of water (brilliant—reload the bladder), and then he commences his king-of-the-parking-lot prance.

"Beautiful dog," calls a voice from across the lot.

I look up and find a man and woman grinning at Henry's imperious look-at-me trot. "Uh, thanks."

"How old is he?" the woman says.

"About ten months."

The man nods. "Still a puppy then. What long legs."

I nod back. He plainly does have long legs.

Right about then, Alan and the boys return. The couple offers a cheery wave, calls a final "good-lookin' dog," and goes on their way.

I wave back, then turn to Alan. "Henry's collecting fans."

"I see that."

An hour and a half later we hit a rest area, and the whole process repeats itself. Alan tears out of the car, dragging two reluctant, empty-bladdered children while I head for a lonely little patch of forest with Henry, the maniac marker.

"Beautiful dog," says a voice from two trees over.

I about jump out of my shoes. Someone else is roaming here? I whip my head around to face a leather-jacketed, nervous-looking man whose bearing makes me think: *America's Most Wanted*.

"Uh, thanks." I try to believe he's a friendly dog walker rather than a serial killer choosing a victim.

Hmm. No dog.

I sneak a peek at Henry.

Great. Peeing on a pine. What's the point of having a viciously fanged protector if he's not going to recognize a potential psycho?

"What is he, a boxer?" The man saunters closer.

"Yeah." Come on, Henry. Show him some teeth.

"I had a couple of boxers."

Had? Past tense is never good when you're dealing with a possible hatchet murderer.

I edge away. "Two, huh?"

Henry buries his nose in the ground cover and tries to inhale the entire earth.

The man chuckles. "Look at those legs. He sure is a good-lookin' dog." Then he flicks a cigarette from his fingers, squashes it in the dirt, and strolls away.

Okay, so maybe he's not a scary killer. Maybe he's just a nice guy enjoying the shade. I ought to stop watching the news.

We finish up bathroom break number two and move on. I'll spare you the details of break number three and only say that it progresses in much the same fashion, except for the added complication of a motion-sick child.

About a mile from my parents' house, Henry stands up, sticks his nose in the air, and starts sniffing like a Hoover vacuum. How does he know we're near our destination?

Alan performs another slam park job in my parents' driveway, and we all pile out. Henry strains at his leash, trying to run every direction at once. What to piddle on first?

After exploring the driveway and a few trees across the street, Henry follows me into the house, where my folks have installed a new wood floor. I'd worried his nails might scratch the wood, so the day before I meticulously trimmed his nails and even sanded them with a power tool—an adventure that required Alan to bodily pin Henry down while I worked the instruments of torture.

When Henry hits the planks, he makes a beeline for my mom. I listen carefully for the click-clack of nails on the wood.

Nothing. Yay, me.

Then I hear the splitter-splatter of urine.

Not so yay.

As an added bonus to christening the floor, he irrigates my mom's shoes, to say nothing of her feet, which are in said shoes.

I cross my arms. "Way to make a first impression, Henry. You had plans of being invited back?"

He wags his stubby tail.

We decide he ought to spend some time on the back deck. Built high in the air, with stairs—which we block—leading down to the yard, it offers a perfect vantage point for Henry to view the world. He bustles back and forth, wholly occupied with the notion that he commands the entire neighborhood. Lake included.

The swimmers two houses down don't care. The squirrels skittering in the trees care only enough to ridicule him with their chatter. The hummingbirds zooming around the feeders care at red-alert level. They launch an all-out offensive and buzz his rear flank.

He would have turned on them, but a bigger problem hurtles onto the scene. A very large, noisy *thing* screeches across the lake. Henry's lake. It comes directly toward him. Sort of.

Henry stiffens, every muscle bulging.

The *thing* keeps coming.

Henry growls deep in his throat, then erupts with his best "I will slash you and tear you" bark.

The thing looms, pauses, as if suddenly seeing Henry's strong lines, his terrible jaws.

Or possibly the people aboard are merely looking for a waterfront restaurant.

Unflinching, Henry glares.

With a roar, the big, noisy thing turns tail and howls away. Henry throws back his head and struts his victory across the deck. Reality is not important in his world.

My mom plops onto a lounge chair. "I'll stay out here with Henry if you want to go in and get settled."

"Okay, thanks."

That's where I leave the scene, but my mom later reports that Henry has a wonderful time trotting around the deck, ogling every moving thing, dead or alive.

Then he sees the flapping leaves on a tree alongside the deck.

They ripple. They flutter.

They *call* to him.

Exactly how he fits his big body through the skinny opening in the railing is a mystery.

My mom flies to the door and proclaims, "The dog jumped off the deck."

No one moves. We merely gape and wonder if we've heard correctly.

"The dog jumped *off the deck*," she enunciates.

Ah. That makes it clear.

Two possibilities hit me. One, he managed to jump near the house where the slope of the yard would make the fall no more than five feet or so, in which case he's likely on his way to Nebraska, or at the very least to the nearby woods, where we'll probably never find him. Or two, he jumped off the end farthest from the house, fell a decent way, crashed into the rock wall at the deck's base, and is lying in a tangled, bloody heap.

Alan and the boys head for the stairs. I scramble to the edge of the deck and peer down.

Did I mention a third possibility?

That Henry would be standing in the yard alive and well, wondering how in the world he got there?

That's where we find him.

A miracle? He flew?

Not exactly. I estimate his trajectory from takeoff. A giant holly bush looms dead center. I can only guess he landed somewhere in the holly bush, crashed through it, and rolled to the ground. The bush appears unharmed.

So, maybe a little miracle. There just happened to be a sturdy holly bush where Henry happened to fall. I like to call these things "God-incidents" as opposed to coincidence. But that's another story.

Meanwhile, we search Henry for wounds. He sports a nice big scratch across his belly and a few small cuts on his legs, but otherwise survives to leap another day.

The next day, to be exact. But this time it isn't from the deck.

I finish lacing my shoes and stand. "I'm going to take Henry for a walk."

My mom stands too. "I'll go with. I always want to walk, but your father never does."

I can see why Mom likes to walk in her neighborhood. She has a forest on one side of the street and a lake on the other. It's beautiful. On the other hand, my dad is no idiot. The place is surrounded by cliffs—er, hills—and you'd better prepare for some serious huffing and puffing if you want to make it to the end of the street.

At the first mention of "walk," Henry jerks to full alert. Cliffs, hills, Himalayas—it's all the same to him.

I snap the leash on Henry's collar. "Let's go."

We barely make it out the door before Henry leaps ahead.

I tug his leash. *"Foose."*

Mom's eyebrows hike. "Foose?"

"It's German—well, German-*ish*—for 'heel.' The trainer says we can't let Henry walk ahead of us. Whenever he tries, we have to correct him with a command and a yank."

Amazingly, Henry stops and waits until we catch up, at which point he darts ahead again.

I jerk the leash. "Foose!"

Henry stops, waits, and then bursts ahead.

This time I get both arms fully into my tug. "FOOSE!"

Henry's head snaps around, and a look of wonder shoots through his wide eyes.

Ah, he knows I mean business. We pull even with him, and he dances at my side.

For all of twenty yards.

But there's so much new stuff to see, smell, and tinkle on. Pretty soon he shakes with anticipation, and his dance becomes a barely contained desire to bolt.

I apply another correction, not as hard as the last—just a reminder that I still command the troops.

For twenty more yards we walk on the ragged edge of mayhem.

Then a S-Q-U-I-R-R-E-L sprints across the street.

Fifty-five pounds of muscled dog bursts into leaping, howling pursuit.

I instinctively plant my feet and leverage my body.

When the slack in Henry's leash runs out, he rebounds like he's just slammed into an invisible wall. That's when the part of his mind where his obedience training lives turns to complete mush. An ordinary dog, after such a monumental yank, might respond with at least some small hesitation.

Not Henry.

Must. Get. Squirrel.

I struggle to rein in Henry's half-witted hulk. He pays as much attention to me as he would to a savage butterfly. This calls for the mother of all corrections.

I reset my body, ready both arms, count to one, and yank for all I'm worth.

My mistimed effort manages little more than a hard pull, and strangulation has never deterred Henry.

If there were a game show called *Stubborn for Dollars*, Henry would be the perpetual champion like that guy on *Jeopardy* who won three million bucks. Then I'd find some comfort in this dim-witted dog and his death-defying obsessions.

Instead, I plot how to crack through his brain freeze and give him a grip on reality. One, I'm not letting go of the leash. Two, he's not going to crash through the forest, chasing some minuscule rodent. And three, even if I do consent to the rodent routine, he doesn't have a prayer of catching it because by now it's certainly at the top of some tree a hundred yards away.

Maybe I need to create slack before I can achieve a suitably devastating yank. I set my feet again and let my arms go forward. Then I squeeze the leash in a death grip and heave with every fiber of my being.

I catch Henry at the pinnacle of his highest leap yet. He performs a spectacular midair tumble, then smacks the pavement. Fanny-first.

Oops.

For an entire second, everything stops.

Then Henry hops up, wipes the astonished look off his face, and trots over to me in his best model-of-obedience persona, as if the squirrel incident never happened.

Truly this dog is missing half his marbles.

I check him over for injuries. Again.

A big red scrape decorates his backside. Now we have to go around explaining why our dog has road rash on his rear. Does fur grow back or will this dog be completely bald by age five?

Henry gives me an enthusiastic "Hey, how 'bout we go for a walk?" look.

I scan our surroundings. We've made it all of two houses from my folks' place. What are the chances we'll make it to the end of the road without seven or eight more leaping death spins?

Nil. But Henry's eyes brim with hope, and his body twitches with sheer love of *the walk*. Sniffing. Marking. Critter chasing. Ah, the joy of the beckoning wilderness. How can I deny him?

I glance at my mom. Her eyes hold the same eagerness. She doesn't get out much.

I wrap the leash around my hand and grip it like a bull rider in the chute. I'm clearly doomed to this jaunt, but hey, here's a happy thought: I've got fifty-fifty odds of making it home without dislocating my shoulder.

7

Henry's view of swimming can be summed up in the following phrase: no stinking way.

We have an inkling of this when we try to give him his first bath. Or shall I say, when we drag his rigid body to the tub and plop our mortified dissenter into the water. After several unsuccessful escape attempts, he switches tactics and pierces our hearts with his last-act-before-burning-at-the-stake martyr gaze.

Unfortunately, Henry happens to have smelly genes. In other words, he stinks. Regularly.

I'm not talking about his gaseous episodes, though I'm certain he could light up an entire county. I'm talking about getting a whiff of this poor dog's natural state. The boxer of my childhood was lucky if he got a bath twice a year, and I never remember an odor billowing from him.

Henry, on the other hand, doesn't have the nickname Stinky Dog for nothing. One week after a bath, we begin to realize he needs another, but we don't want to traumatize him so soon. Two weeks later, he's living on borrowed time. After three weeks? Get your water wings, bucko, it's time for splashdown.

Sometimes we're too busy to stop the world for heinous water torture, and we endure *Le Nasty Dog Bouquet* for upwards of a month. That's where we always draw the line, and the bathtub of doom claims its victim.

So when Jacob and Jonathan go down to the dock at my parents' house to swim, they have no luck getting Henry to join the splashing fun. That's not to say he doesn't have a jolly time. Oh, the thrill of trouncing around the dock, barking at every bird, boat, and harmless piece of driftwood.

Naturally we block the dock's ramp so he can't run off through everyone's yard. It's not that he doesn't like us and constantly tries to run away. It's that sudden freedom makes him lose his mind, so we try not to burden him with it.

Did I say we blocked the ramp? Make that, we thought we blocked it. After ten minutes of yapping and prancing, Henry discovers an opening.

Poof.

In less than half a second, Henry accelerates to ain't-no-catching-him speed. He tears across the yard and barrels halfway through the neighbor's lawn before the wet grass sweeps away his feet like a rampaging rhino hitting a Slip 'n Slide.

Personally, I think any major leaguer barreling toward home plate would be jealous of the sheer speed and distance Henry so effortlessly covers in his full-bodied skid, to say nothing of his guaranteed-to-slam-a-catcher senseless momentum. Fortunately, no collision meets the end of his slide. He simply staggers to his feet, a look of "What in the world happened?" plastered on his face.

As humans with comparatively inferior acceleration, we'd just made it off the dock's ramp by then.

"Henry, you wanna treat?" Jonathan calls.

Henry stands, clearly undecided. Should he run for it?

Jacob and I repeat the dog-speak key word. "Treat!"

Henry turns away, gazing at the freedom of the open yards all lined up side by side. So much to smell . . .

Jonathan waves his empty hand. "I've got cheese, Henry." Does it count as a lie if the lie-ee isn't human?

Jacob waves too. "Cheese, Henry."

Swell. The whole family is morphing into a bunch of two-faced fibbers.

Henry shifts his weight but doesn't bolt. He's particularly fond of cheese.

There's only one thing to do. I run to the house to scrounge for cheddar. The boys can probably keep Henry in their sights while I snatch the bribe.

By the time I make it back outside, the boys have captured Henry. They're obviously convincing liars. Disturbing, really, yet undeniably helpful at the moment.

Another inspection of Henry's body follows.

"Thanks to your Ty Cobb routine, you're minus a big fur patch on your left leg. That whole bald thing? You've got three years tops."

Henry wags his tail and gulps the cheese.

"Assuming you make it to age three. Let's get you back to the dock."

This time I double-check the blockade.

The boys slap their life jackets on and race for the end of the dock. In true boy fashion, they hurl themselves into the air, gyrate wildly, and hit the water in the most reckless way possible. After which, they climb out and repeat the process ad infinitum.

Henry scampers after every flying boy, except he screeches to a halt about half an inch from the dock's edge.

Right. How long before this ends in disaster?

Um, not long.

One of the reasons the boys get such height on their aerials is because the dock is a good thirty inches above the water. One slight miscalculation later, Henry finds himself hanging in midair.

Two thoughts flash through my mind. First, Henry's about to

experience a distinctly unpleasant surprise. And second, can he swim?

Granted, a bad time to be asking.

Henry crashes through the water's surface like a comet hitting the ocean, then he comes up sputtering.

Surely he can doggie paddle?

Let me bear witness: no.

Instead he performs a gasping, choking, help-me-I'm-drowning thrash.

We panic. How do you get a fifty-five-pound, drowning dog out of the water with the dock nearly three feet up and the shore fifty feet away?

The boys scream, sure their dog is a goner.

I do the only thing I can do. I slap on a life jacket and plunge in.

One word about the water temperature. Cold.

Scratch that. Insanely cold.

Like, why-in-the-world-am I letting-my-kids-swim-in-it cold.

I paddle toward Henry.

His erratic thrash sends him the opposite direction.

Great, because I wanted to swim around the whole lake to save my dog.

A couple of big waves crash against Henry's head and knock him in yet another direction. How can any dog be so inept at swimming? Isn't it an instinct for canines?

I ditch my plan to get him to shore. We don't have all day. A few fancy maneuvers on my part, and I get near enough for his flailing legs to scrape against me.

That's when his instinct kicks in, only it isn't the swimming one. It's climbing, and I'm the handiest thing for him to climb.

Thank God for my life jacket.

We slosh in the waves as Henry attempts to scramble aboard the SS *Erin*. This works about as well as an elephant climbing a floating beach ball. Of course, elephants swim better than Henry, so I suppose that's irrelevant.

In case you don't know about life jackets, let me explain that they prevent you from becoming a permanent part of the lake bottom, but any type of force, like, say, a panicked dog clawing up your stomach, can still bob your nose under. A lot.

I spew lake water from my mouth. "Get him to the ladder, boys."

Working together, we herd Henry toward the ladder on the dock.

You probably see the flaw in my plan. Henry can do many things, but climbing up a swim ladder isn't one of them.

My feet find a rung but promptly slip off. I hook an arm around the ladder to steady myself. Then I have to figure out how to push fifty-five pounds of dog three feet into the air. Using one hand.

Doesn't happen.

Alan arrives and reaches down to help. I push, Henry claws, Alan heaves, and somehow we get our sodden doggie to safety.

I scramble out close behind.

Poor Henry doesn't know what to do first, so he runs around the dock, doing a full-body shimmy every three steps. There I sit, cold, soppy, and huddled in a teensy towel while Henry showers us with ice water. I want to wring his scrawny, can't-swim-worth-beans neck, but he looks more miserable than I do.

Ten minutes later, he resumes the chasing of leaping children. Is there no brain cell he can devote to memory?

Apparently not. He edges ever closer to another unplanned plunge.

That's when I decide swim time is over. "Okay, guys. You need to get out."

"W-w-why?" Jacob's blue lips can barely move.

Gee, I don't know. Hypothermia maybe? "We've been out here long enough. You don't want Henry to fall in again, do you?"

Guilt. Much better than arguing about how cold the boys aren't.

We make our way back to the house and meet my dad coming out on the deck.

"You missed all the excitement," Mom tells him. "Henry fell in the lake."

"Fell?"

I hang my towel over the railing. "Yeah, but we fished him out."

"He can't swim?"

Sure he can swim. Like a fifty-five-pound cat.

I plop on a chair. "I don't know what we're going to do. I can't be bringing him down to the dock when he's a drowning hazard."

"You could get him a life jacket."

"A life jacket? For a dog?"

Dad shrugs. "Sure. They make 'em. What if a dog fell off a boat in the middle of the ocean or something?"

The next day Alan troops to the store. We each have our special gifts, and Alan's much better at buying ridiculously overpriced things without getting snarky. You can get your kid a life jacket for all of ten bucks, but some company slaps a canine label on the same basic parts—cheap foam and nylon straps—and you're forking over thirty-five smackers. It's like a tax on people who own clumsy dogs.

And do these life jackets actually work? In all my visits to the lake, I've yet to see another canine clothed in one. For all I know, this is just some brilliant moneymaking scheme. Where else is a life jacket company going to find a new market niche?

Worse than paying thirty-five dollars for a doggie-jacket that theoretically works is paying thirty-five bucks for one that doesn't.

There's only one thing to do. Test the jacket.

On Henry.

In the water.

Make that, in the shallow water. Just in case.

The next day arrives with perfect weather. We wait until the afternoon sun gives the lake its peak warmth. Then it's time for Henry to take the plunge.

Not that he knows anything about it.

The boys put on their bathing suits, and Henry perks his ears. Changing clothes means something big is happening.

Then I get out the life jacket, and he glues his nose to it. For him, this is getting better by the moment. First people changing clothes, then a new toy.

I toss in the kicker. "Henry, let's go outside."

He folds himself in half with delight, and I have a flashback to all the times I took my kids for vaccinations with the phrase, "Hey, boys, guess what? We're going to McDonald's to play on the slides, and we only have to make one little stop at the doctor's office first."

Manipulation is a beautiful thing.

When used responsibly.

We troop outside and make a beeline for shore. Henry skips beside us. The boys hit the water and splash in waist-deep. Henry jerks to a halt, then dances in place while the boys call to him.

Ah, distraction. The perfect time to slip on something uncomfortable.

The jacket looks simple enough. If you have a PhD.

Fortunately, Alan does, so we get the thing on before we all die of old age.

Then comes the testing part. Right. How to get him in the water?

I give a little tug on his leash and muster the world's most enthusiastic timbre. "Swim time, Henry. Let's go!"

He glances left and right, clearly mortified.

"You can do it, Henry. It'll be fun."

He turns his head away as if to say, "I'm not that stupid."

I don't blame him. I'm not buying the fun thing either. "Sorry, Henry. We have to test the life jacket. Foose."

Amazing how he can mimic a deaf dog.

I move right in front of him. "I know you heard me. Like it or not, you're going in that lake."

Alan grabs the handle on the back of the life jacket—convenient for pulling a dog out of water, though I doubt anyone ever needed it for the inbound trip—and tugs.

That gets his attention. Henry's eyes go wide in full-blown distress.

Itty bit by itty bit, we coax him toward the lake. We get his toes in, then his forelegs. Soon he's chest deep.

The boys cheer him on.

Henry tucks his tail and pins his ears back. Every feature on his face says, "Make it stop, make it stop, make it stop . . ."

Two more steps and the bottom drops away. Henry's personal floatation device takes over as a real, life-saving, dog-floating piece of foam.

He starts paddling his legs.

"Henry, you're swimming! Good boy!"

Steering, on the other hand, is a foreign concept. He heads out to sea, with a look that says, "This is SO not fun."

I give a gentle tug on the leash, which turns him back toward me. Big mistake, because pretty soon his feet hit the bottom and he tries to run out of the water. But he doesn't stop when his leash goes taut, which forces him sideways, and ultimately into a U-turn.

Mindlessly, he splashes once again into deep water. The life jacket takes over, and he looks up at me with a "How did I get back here?" face.

"It's still swim time, Henry. There is no escape."

He shoots me a long-suffering look. The same kind I'm giving him.

"Listen, mister, we forked out thirty-five bucks for that thing. You're not getting out before we know whether it'll hold together for more than five minutes." Then I soften. "It's for your own safety. And you never know. You might start to like swimming."

Right. When cheese rains from the sky.

You'd think that when we take Henry for his first boat ride, we'd slap on that expensive life jacket and get our money's worth. Um, no. We forget it.

I'm still miffed about that. For thirty-five bucks, I don't know why the thing can't play a song like those dancing Santas do when you walk by. Maybe something like the *Gilligan's Island* theme song?

We fire up the pontoon boat and load everyone aboard. Sans doggie life jacket. In our defense, the boat has gates and railings all around it, with the gates being solid on the bottom two-thirds. The upper third is open space topped with another railing. You can't fall off.

We putter, dog and all, across the placid lake. Normal dogs on boat rides seem so . . . normal . . . in comparison to Henry. They sit there and enjoy the trip. Not Henry. He ricochets around the boat like an ADHD toddler hooked on Mountain Dew.

He trots to the front, hangs out his tongue, looks left, looks right, then bustles to the back. Wheedles a pat from my mom, gets a rub from my dad, scampers away from me because I look like I might make him sit still, then hits rigid-bodied alert as another boat cruises by.

After that, he sticks his nose through the gate on the left because there just might be an attack from, say, a wave or something. Then he darts to the gate on the right because some birds fly by, and you never know when they'll turn sinister.

Then Henry dashes to the front and starts the whole circuit again.

And again.

And again.

I roll my eyes and hope the boat's carpet label says "Extra durability for hyperactive dogs." After another ten minutes, I'm ready to tackle Henry and sit on him. We frequently resort to this at home, though Henry seems to consider it a delightful game.

Of course, it's one thing to pin your dog to the ground in the privacy of your own house, and quite another to do it in the middle of a well-populated lake. Even when traffic is light, people still hang out on their docks or porches and watch passing boats. Do I really want to chase my dog from one end of the boat to the other and launch into WrestleMania XXXV in front of a bunch of spectators?

Then Henry's body goes stiff. His eyes fix on something in the distance. My gaze follows his.

Ducks.

Henry knows about ducks. They paddle by my folks' dock every now and again and rile him senseless. I suspect one of those ducks—a three-time mama that can't even fly—torments him on purpose.

Henry darts to the front of the boat and thrusts his nose through the gate. He tries to growl, but it comes out muffled.

Dinner plans? Revenge? He thinks they're plotting piracy?

His recent death leap off the house deck flickers through my mind and raises an inkling of worry. Scratch that. This is a lake. Filled with cold water.

Chances of Henry hurtling himself into the mother of all bathtubs? Nil.

Or so I think.

He sees the ducks. He barks at the ducks. He vaults after the ducks.

It's never a good idea to take a header off the front end of a moving boat, but if you insist on trying, well, it's best if you're inept.

Henry doesn't think to jump *over* the gate because his nose is already stuck through it. Instead, he tries to squirt the rest of his body through the gap and gets momentarily stuck. Just as the upper half of his body springs free, Jonathan, the only person close enough to do anything about it, flings himself forward and grabs Henry's back left leg.

For that one instant, Henry hangs there flailing, Jonathan clutching.

The rest of us burst from our paralyzed shock. Dad cuts the engine. Alan, Jacob, and I race to the front of the boat and haul Henry back through the opening.

Then we sit, agape at what might have been. We have to face reality. Our dog is suicidal.

The boat would have run over him—they don't stop on a dime—and the pontoons on either side would have forced him into the propeller. I mean, who hasn't seen *Indiana Jones* and the famous fight on the tarmac under the airplane's spinning blades? The one where you know what's coming and can't help but watch with morbid anticipation.

Not something you want to re-create on a family vacation.

What made this dog jump after ducks in the middle of the lake when he won't jump off the dock? (*Fall* off the dock, yes. Jump, no.)

My dad starts the boat and whirls it around.

Good plan. Leave the scene of the crime. Preferably before anyone can identify us.

Dad gives me a look somewhere between amusement and pity. "Keep hold of that dog."

Um, yeah.

I grab Henry and force him to stay by me. He looks at me—I think he rolls his eyes—as if I have absolutely no idea how to have fun.

8

If you're going to have a destructive, er . . . energetic pooch, it behooves you to find games and toys to occupy him. That's where all you people with retrievers have the advantage on the rest of us. They come with a built-in instinct for a game that'll wear out your fur-coated power plant.

I know you're going to complain that once you start throwing, there's no end in sight, but at least you don't have to teach your pet to play a constructive game. And hey, it's admirable when a dog will crawl uphill through driving sleet, dragging his two broken legs, to deliver a slobbery ball for the seven billionth throw.

In Henry's puppy days, I decide this whole fetch deal will be good for him. My boxer book reports these dogs don't seem naturally inclined or interested in such a game, but that doesn't deter me. I raid the garage for a tennis ball.

"Henry, let's play ball. Doesn't this look like a nice toy?"

He gives it a sniff.

"Okay, good. Now, I'll toss it and you get it."

With minimal interest, Henry watches it roll by.

"I don't think you're getting the idea here. You're supposed to chase it."

I walk over, pick it up, and roll it right at him.

It bumps into his oversized puppy foot and startles him, as if he had no idea it would hit him. For all of one second, he seems to consider chasing the ricochet.

"Get the ball, Henry." I use my most excited voice.

He turns to me, gives me the haunches-down play posture, and starts to hop at me.

"The ball, Henry." I grab the toy and toss it.

He goes for my pant leg.

Okay, no enthusiasm for the little green ball. Maybe I'll have more success with a different toy.

When we acquired Henry, the breeder sent along a small stuffed animal—shaped like a boxer puppy—that he'd had since he was only a few weeks old. We call it his baby. Henry shows no remorse over mangling every other piece of fabric he comes in contact with, but he never gnaws on his baby. He likes to play tug-of-war with it, though, so I don't know what that says about him.

I snatch up the baby and wave it around. "Hey, Henry, I've got your baby."

That snaps his interest back to the toy rather than me, and he makes a mad dash for it. I pass it from hand to hand, spin around, and finally toss it.

Henry's gangly puppy legs trample after the thing. He clamps his little teeth on it and whirls in triumph.

I clap my hands. "Bring it here, Henry."

If a puppy can laugh with a big stuffed animal crammed in his mouth, Henry appears to do just that. Then he runs off, expecting me to chase him.

Game over.

But we'd made progress. The next time he brings me the baby for tug-of-war, I try to warp it into fetch.

First I have to get it away from him.

"Oos." This is my bad German for "Let go you dumb dog."

He gives me a puppy growl and a look that says, "Hellooo? Tug-of-war is where you hang on till your teeth fall out."

By now, I've had a fair bit of practice getting precious heirlooms and dangerous objects out of his mouth (provided we've caught him before said objects have become unrecognizable bits). I work the baby free.

Henry's gaze fixes on it as if the fate of the universe rests on rewrapping his teeth around the thing and clinging for all eternity.

I whip my hand one way, another way, a third way, and then hurl the baby across the room.

He pounces after it like a crazed jungle cat, attacks, and comes up shaking the poor thing in some primal urge to break its polyester neck.

"You got it, Henry. Good boy! Bring it here."

Instead of coming to me, he prances a victory lap around the living room. Every few steps he shakes the baby so hard he nearly falls over.

I clap my hands, and he turns toward me, his little chest puffed and his head thrust high.

"Here, Henry." I work the applause. "Bring it here."

After a moment of indecision, he trots toward me.

Kneeling down, I clap until he runs into my arms, at which point he smacks into my chest.

How cute is that? He reminds me of a toddler who, after his first run across the room, crashes into his parent's waiting arms.

Of course, then Henry wants to play tug-of-war again.

I comply—briefly—then stick my fingers into his mouth and free the baby. We repeat the waving, tossing, pouncing, shaking, clapping routine, and he thuds into my chest once again.

"Good fetch. You brought your baby." I rub his wriggly little body, and he dances with delight. Then he shoves the baby at me for more tug-of-war. Again I tug for a few moments before taking it away.

Wave, toss, pounce, shake, clap, thud.

Three times in a row. Have I finally taught him something useful?

Um, no. The next time I throw the baby, he decides my shirtsleeve is far more tantalizing. He doesn't even watch the baby sail by.

The next day he forgets the game altogether and doesn't so much as touch his precious toy.

Some days later, I pick it up and toss it hand to hand. "Henry, let's play with your baby."

His eyes say, "Oh boy! Let's play with your sweatshirt!" Then he pounces.

I ought to give up, but no, I'm determined to teach him to fetch. The following day, he brings me his baby. His eyes and body language say, "You vill play tug-of-var vit me." German accent and all.

I take advantage of his stubbornness. For a few moments, I tug. Then I peel it from his mouth and go through the whole waving, tossing routine. He brings the baby to me again and again, certain we'll have a rousing tussle. I barely pull before I take it and toss it again, each time a little farther.

Each time, he scampers back and crashes into my body. It's seriously adorable. He can't control his puppy legs well enough to avoid slamming me.

After several days of Fetch and Slam, I notice Henry deliberately lowers his head and turns it at the last instant so he can barrel his shoulder into me. Apparently he thinks crashing is part of the game.

Still, it's so gangly and cute that I don't think it through. Unlike normal boxers, Henry isn't a cuddly dog. He doesn't try to sit in your lap or lie on your feet or anything like that. I think he goes out of his way to hide so he can perpetrate evil deeds.

This crashing business is probably his way of initiating friendly contact, like two football players doing the midair chest bump. I don't discourage it—these brief moments of connection are all we have.

But you know where this is going.

Henry plays Fetch and Slam with me month after month after month. Next thing I know, I've got sixty-five pounds of dog plowing across the living room to slam me with the mother of all body checks.

I couldn't have just taught him to play dead dog?

Henry's baby lasts well over two years. Then one day he turns on it. Snatches it, runs around with it awhile, then sits down and tears it to pieces. I don't know why. I don't understand the fascination with eating the stuffing, either, but he's gulping down the polyester when I discover him.

The incident dooms poor baby—what's left of it—to the garbage. No way am I going to get stuck calling the vet to confess my dog ate an entire stuffed animal.

We try to play fetch with a tennis ball, but that doesn't work out too well. Henry still thinks tug-of-war is a necessary part of the game. As if I'll stick my hand in his big mouth and try to yank out a slimy ball caged in teeth?

I look around the house for something with a little more substance, i.e., something big enough to hang outside his mouth, and discover most of Henry's toys in a state of near consumption. What in the world is wrong with this dog? Does he have some vendetta against all things plastic?

Our house is death row for squeakies. Yet he loves them with a passion most exuberant. Here's our family on Christmas morning:

We sit around the Christmas tree in the middle of the house. To keep Henry busy, he gets the first present—a new toy. He takes a sniff, clamps his teeth on it—SQUEAK—then leaps up and runs to one end of the house.

Zoom, squeak, squeak, squeak

He whips around, passes us, and dashes to the other end of the house.

Zoom, squeak, squeak, squeak

Then the rest of us open our stockings.

Zoom, squeak, squeak, squeak

Then we open presents.

Zoom, squeak, squeak, squeak

Have coffee.

Zoom, squeak, squeak, squeak

Breakfast.

Zoom, squeak, squeak, squeak

This goes on all morning. Henry is incurably happy.

Eventually he gets tired of running, so he lies down and chomps away on the toy while it goes *squeak squeak squeak*. Every so often he lifts his head and howls. Yes, howls. Like a wolf. Once that long wail soars to the sky, you can pretty much kiss Mr. Squeaky good-bye.

One day we find an extra-sturdy, rubberized, squeaky gorilla. Despite the high cost, we buy it. Henry adores the thing. It has some kind of foam inside to give it more substance when he clamps his teeth on it.

Alas, a few weeks later he plops down and gnaws its hands off. Not the head, not the feet. Just the hands. This wouldn't have been so bad, but then he starts pulling out the foam for breakfast.

Good-bye, gorilla. It gets a one-way ticket to the trash.

Poor thing ought to have had a funeral service or something, because Henry can't cope with the loss. Day after day he roams the house, sniffing and whining. So what does Alan do? He buys another one. Same exact eight-dollar ape. This from the man with a PhD.

An hour later the unfortunate gorilla is handless and headed for the garbage.

Our dog kills more toys than a pack of pillaging preschoolers, but I still feel sorry for him. He wants to play sooooo badly.

The next time I buy something new, I get the brilliant plan to monitor Henry's play. When he turns destructive, I kidnap Mr. Squeaky.

Henry launches a frantic search and rescue mission, only I don't think the rescue part will end well for Mr. Squeaky. After hours of sniffing, Henry's nose tells him I'm harboring the toy atop the fireplace mantel.

Several minutes of staring and whining achieve nothing, so Henry launches himself at the mantel—claws first. He misses the toy, but his nails rake the wood, leaving long, jagged streaks through the oak. For pity's sake, people are going to think we're harboring a pack of trolls here.

My next brilliant plan is to make searching for extra-durable squeakies part of my shopping routine. One day I happen upon a thick, squeaking ball. For sure it can withstand Henry's teeth. Maybe.

I plunk it on the checkout counter in front of the clerk. "Do you know anything about the company that makes this ball?"

She looks the toy over. "I don't recognize the brand, but it seems sturdy." "Yeah, that's what we thought about the last toy we bought. It was expensive, and our dog destroyed it." I didn't mention we'd been dumb enough to buy two.

"Did you save the receipt? You could have brought it back if it was defective or something."

Did having chew-offable hands qualify as defective?

"I'm not sure the problem was with the *toy* exactly. My dog is pretty hard on stuff. I'm worried he'll ruin this ball."

She squeezes it. "Feels pretty strong. I can't imagine you'll have any trouble, but if you do, just bring it back."

"You mean if he chews the thing to pieces, I can actually return it?"

Her eyebrows hitch, as if she can't possibly call up an image of this ball in pieces. Then she offers a perhaps-you're-a-little-too-paranoid smile. "Just save the receipt."

I save it. Good thing. After twenty minutes of delirious joy, Henry kills the ball. Bites the squeaky right out of it and leaves a one-inch hole.

I head back to the store. Of course the checkout gal remembers me. I'd been there half an hour ago. As she inspects the ball, her head keeps tilting sideways, like she needs another angle to actually believe what she's seeing. The nice hole makes the thickness of the rubber apparent. I'll say this, the gal wasn't wrong in thinking the ball would be sturdy. She'd just underestimated Henry.

"Why don't you see if you can find something else?" Her voice has a good-luck-with-that tone.

Up and down the aisles I troop. Then a football-shaped toy catches my gaze. It's made from the material of a tennis ball. Might be just the thing. Henry has yet to rip up a tennis ball. Of course, he never shows much interest in them, either.

But this one squeaks. And bounces in funny, unpredictable directions.

I take it home and give it to Henry.

Ha! It takes a good hour or two before he kills the squeaker function, but the toy remains intact.

He runs, he shakes, he tosses, he chomps, he howls.

The toy lives.

Then a little piece of green fuzz comes loose from the rubber. It dangles seductively.

For days, Henry systematically skins the fuzz off the ball. Soon it's a barely recognizable, half-naked rubber thing with soggy green tentacles—his favorite toy.

Alas. There comes a day—you know there has to—when he tears the rubber apart. I've saved the receipt, but honestly, Henry's gotten weeks of entertainment out of that football. I don't feel justified demanding my money back.

Still, we can't keep spending all this cash on toys condemned to death.

New plan: cheap, disposable toys.

One day I find a big, plastic, squeaky pencil at the grocery store. A dollar-forty-seven. Perfect. Even if Henry only gets a day out of it.

But why, why, why am I a sucker for this dog? I don't even like him. Why do I feel sorry for his dumb fetishes that lead to his dumb predicaments that cause his dumb grief?

I buy the stinkin' toy.

He kills the squeak in record time—I haven't even finished putting the groceries away. That spells impending doom for the pencil. Another doggie dollar sucked out of the family budget in less than twenty minutes.

And yet, Henry doesn't rip into the rubber. He doesn't even try.

He trashes expensive toys one after another.

Buy him something cheap . . .

He keeps it forever.

9

I t's funny how a new-construction neighborhood works. Everyone wants to meet everyone so they can form a tight-knit community. People are always out checking the progress of different houses and the amenity developments.

Our family, for instance, monitors the growth of the paved walking trails. Incessantly. Because we're always on them. Alan walks Henry, I walk Henry, Jacob and Jonathan walk Henry.

While Henry's unquenchable exercise needs are a nuisance, at least it gets our family out among the crowd of new homeowners. When they see us coming, Henry's charisma makes their faces break into big, shiny grins. "Hey, there's Henry. Hi, Henry!"

Then they stop and pet him. I think the attention energizes him and locks his stamina tank on perpetual full.

I'm not the best person at putting a name to a face, so I don't mind when people forget who I am, but when the whole neighborhood knows your dog's name long before they've got yours mastered, what does that say?

One day Henry and I meet two neighbors walking their Weimaraner. I don't remember their names, but at least I don't know their dog's name either. They know Henry, though.

I step forward for a brief chat, not paying much attention to Henry's rowdy misbehavior and impertinent leash-tugging behind me. The couple chuckles and looks past me. I turn around and come eyeball to eyeball with my dog, who's three feet in the air like a ridiculous jumping bean. I didn't even know he could jump that high. Apparently this is his new sign language for "Oh, play with me, play with me, please, please, PLEASE!"

The couple and their dog go on their way. Snickering. Even the dog.

Henry doesn't care. He keeps hopping as if any second they'll change their minds and come frolic with him.

He seems to harbor the same BFF enthusiasm for every new person or dog he meets. Until the day we drive home from a hectic road trip.

Jonathan starts throwing up ninety miles from our house, and erupts at least four times before we hit the outskirts of our town. Normally we're prepared for a barfing incident or two on trips, but this challenges our resources. He never gives us more than three seconds' warning, and with the turnpike's speed limit of seventy-five, slamming the brakes so our kid can puke out the window would probably roll the car. Instead, he fills our emergency sandwich bags, a Walmart bag, and Alan's empty Pepsi cup. By the time we roll into our driveway, I figure Jonathan's upchucked every milliliter of fluid in his body.

Nope. He gets that look in his eye, and a little groan escapes his lips. In the midst of the commotion, no one thinks to close the garage door.

I settle Jonathan in his bed, with a barf cup by his side, and then go check if Alan needs more help unpacking. All the doors stand open, and I can see out to the street, where a young couple pushes a stroller past our house. They have a cute yellow Labrador retriever trotting alongside. I barely form a hmm-I-don't-recognize-them thought before Henry streaks past like a brown bullet.

Despite Alan's shouts and the couple's startled gasps, Henry launches himself at their dog. Alan sprints to the street and yanks Henry away by the back legs. The poor Lab totters backward, wearing a bewildered look. His owners give us the same look.

What can we say after that? Welcome to the neighborhood?

Alan pours out a stream of apologies as he drags Henry to the house. I just stand there with my mouth gaping. Henry treats the other four-legged residents of this neighborhood as lifelong buddies, so why harass this particular dog? Baby stroller phobia?

I ask Angel about it the next time I see him.

"Sometimes a dog can develop a dislike for another dog and transfer it to the whole species," Angel tells me. "Maybe there was a yellow Lab somewhere that Henry didn't get along with."

"I don't remember him meeting any before this one."

"We kennel yellow Labs occasionally. Maybe one was here the same time as Henry. Sometimes dogs can get into kennel wars, where they bark and do aggressive posturing. Henry could remember something like that."

Another psychological anomaly for Henry. Retriever rage. Yellows only.

"What about the baby stroller? Could that have freaked him out?"

Angel gives a half nod. "I guess it's possible. Without having seen his behavior, it's hard to say."

A few days later, I hear about a dog park within driving distance. Sounds like a smash idea. Henry can exhaust himself running in a big open space, and I can save some miles on my legs. But I'll have to watch for signs of retriever rage.

Henry and I find the place easily enough. His nose quivers as I park the car, and his body breaks out in an excited shimmy. I barely manage to rein him in as we approach the tall fence surrounding the play area.

"Foose, Henry. You're not going in there before I get a chance to look this over."

Through the chain-link fence, I see a zoo of dog breeds romping every which way. Owners mill around chatting, hurling tennis balls, and scooping periodic doggie droppings into well-placed garbage cans.

A couple of black retrievers dash past us. Henry leaps for the sky, as if that'll make them come play with him. They don't even slow down. Then a small mix of something-or-other breed runs right to the fence in front of us. Her cute little brown nose pokes through the links. Henry rears up with another "Play with me" leap. The mixed breed bows in play posture, then runs off.

Henry tries to follow, but the fence and the leash kill his plan.

He shoots me a look that says, "How come everyone else gets to play?"

"No, Henry. Not till I'm sure you'll behave in there."

Over the next few minutes, an assortment of dogs scampers past Henry's eager nose. He greets each with total thrill, then progressively more whining as they trot off without him. I feel like I've brought a kid to Disney World and told him to sit in the car.

Then a yellow Lab happens by. Before I can cringe, Henry breaks into his "Play with me" routine. So much for retriever rage. Either he inexplicably hates the one Lab in our neighborhood or he has a case of stroller phobia.

"All right, Henry. We can give this a try."

Through the gates of the doggie Magic Kingdom, a huge expanse of weakly grassed turf opens before us. I keep Henry on leash and survey the host of cavorting dogs. No fighting, no bickering.

Henry dances and whimpers, clearly all play.

Far ahead, the ground rolls a little and hides the other end of the park, but it seems safe enough.

I let Henry off the leash, and immediately a couple of yellow Labs come running.

Henry coils and bursts into his most joyous leap yet. Then he dashes off with his new pals.

I stroll along the walkway and watch Henry frisk to and fro, greeting—nicely—every dog and person he finds. On the far side of the scraggly wannabe turf, a narrow lagoon juts deep into the park. The possibility of a lake area had never occurred to me. What a great deal for all the water dogs. They splash through the lagoon's shallows and plunge across its depths, chasing balls, each other, and the pure joy of wetness.

One drawback—the dog traffic stamps out the last hope of grass. Mud mess reigns.

Henry follows a couple of retrievers to the edge and looks distastefully at his soggy feet. I can almost see his mind working. *"Eeew. Water. Hey, what are those guys doing running into that stuff? They went off and left me . . ."*

A woman standing nearby turns to me. "Is that your boxer?"

I pull my gaze from Henry. "Yeah."

"He sure is pretty."

"Thanks."

I'm about to ask which dog is hers when a soaking setter lumbers up and deposits a sodden ball at her feet. She picks it up and tosses it into the lagoon. The dog plows past Henry, spraying him with grimy water.

Lovely. He'll need a bath now.

The woman nods in Henry's direction. "Does your dog like to swim?"

"Oh, no."

"I thought boxers loved the water."

"Not Henry. He hates it."

My mud-speckled dog stands a moment longer, then trots right into the lake.

I'm sure the lady wears a suitably piteous look for poor, deluded me, but I'm too stunned to care. "That's not . . . he wouldn't . . . how can . . ."

Henry doesn't just walk a little way in. He keeps right on going and tries to swim.

I watch him flounder. Just how deep is the water?

Henry paddles chaotically until he finds himself in the middle of the lagoon. Then he suddenly seems to realize he's trying to swim. Badly. His head bobs under, then pops up.

Thrash. Writhe. Panic.

My dog's gonna drown.

Or I'm gonna splash into that cold muddy mess and save him.

He flails past the midpoint, so I now have to hightail it to the other side of the lagoon. While it stretches only fiftyish feet across, it's twice as long. I huff my way around the shore, keeping Henry locked in my sights and trying to steel myself for a rescue.

Just when I make it, panting, to the other side, I catch the look on his face.

Mindless shock. His eyes seem to focus on nothing, as if his entire head were merely a container of vacant space.

I'm one step from plunging in when an odd determination laces into his face. A dawning look of "Hey, I hate water. I'm getting out of here."

He's made it two-thirds of the way across, but his brilliant conclusion leads him to turn right around and go back the way he came.

"Henry, no! You're going . . . never mind." My voice dies to a mutter. He shows no signs of hearing me.

Henry's newfound resolution energizes him back to the halfway point, but his head still rides low in the water. Too low.

I peel off on another pell-mell lap around the lagoon. When I reach the original side where the lady stands—probably gaping, though I don't dare meet her eye—Henry still wears his stubborn look. That's when I know the most graceless swimmer on earth will live to thrash another day.

His feet find the muddy bottom. He scrambles ashore, shakes himself, and hustles away from all semblance of wet ground.

Our first delightful day at the dog park.

10

I wish I knew what makes Henry so perpetually aloof. The boxer of my childhood couldn't bear to sit across the room from me, much less across the house. With Henry, all I have is Fetch and Slam. Oh, the tenderness.

To be fair, it's not like he isn't happy when we come home. He trots all wiggly-diggly to us and curves his body into undulating *S* shapes. Then he runs to the door as if the sole purpose of our coming home is to take him for a walk. If that fails, he brings a toy for tug-of-war. If that fails, he disappears into another room and forgets about us.

Unless someone happens to have a strange new item. If Henry is one part lunatic, and one part energy overdrive, the rest of the pie chart has to be pure curiosity. Socket wrench? Fascinating. Ice pick? Enthralling. Battery acid? Lemme at it.

The best item of all? Car keys. Every jingle makes Henry fly to the door and stand there looking at us expectantly. Heaven help us if we're just moving our keys and don't plan to go anywhere.

Whenever standing at the door fails to bring immediate action, Henry changes tactics. He follows me through the house to make sure I don't sneak off without him. If my going-away routine progresses—the shoes, the purse, the coat—his exuberant anticipation reaches maximum bounce, and he wriggles with departure delirium.

As if I want him along for my root canal.

The possibility that he's staying home never dawns on him. Not until I'm closing the door in his face. Then he hits me with those pathetic "Oh please take me with you" eyes. How do I turn that down? And I know full well he just likes the car. It's not that he wants to be with me or anything noble like that.

Alas. I take the dog along every place halfway appropriate. Video store? He comes. Gas station? He's there. Quick grocery trip? You betcha.

Not that he's well behaved during the ride. Picture a Ping-Pong ball in a tiny wind tunnel set to hurricane speed.

One day a little car trip creates a new problem. Henry and I come home after dropping Jacob off at church—a very short trip. I open the back door for Henry to get out, but he just stands there looking at me.

I motion to him. "Come on. We're all done."

Blank stare.

"You're just going to stand there?"

Apparently so.

"Well, I'm going in."

And so I do. But I leave the car door open and crack the door to the house. I take off my coat, put away my keys and wallet.

No Henry.

I peek out the door to check on him.

There he is, right where I left him in the car. Like if he just stands there long enough, I'll come back and take him for another ride.

Shoot me, somebody, when I become my doggie's chauffeur.

You might not believe this, but after Henry's first fun-filled visit to the lake, we dare to bring him back several more times. He does, in fact, fall off the dock on every single visit. Never wearing the life jacket.

I think the neighbors are on to the show. Whenever they see a maniac boxer hopping around the dock, they run for their binoculars. We're better than cable TV.

All right, I've never actually seen them with binocs, but I wouldn't blame them.

At least we're getting pretty good at fishing Henry out. After that, the boys always beg us to wrangle his life jacket on him. Of course, then he never falls.

Actually, as he's picked up some fat, er . . . weight, he's improved his swimming stroke. I can safely say he's gone from utterly inept to merely horrible. I think if he keeps plunging away, he'll one day graduate to fairly bad.

He hasn't set another paw on the pontoon boat, but we're okay with that. Then comes the day my mom strolls down to the dock and announces she wants to take him for a ride in the bass boat.

Dad and I had just docked it after fishing all morning. He wrinkles his brow. "You want to take the dog for a bass-boat ride?"

Mom doesn't bat an eye. "Yes."

"I'm supposed to take off the padlock, unchain the boat, unplug the battery charger, lower the lift, and put the boat back in the water so you can take the dog for a ride?"

"Erin can come too."

Because I've forgotten what a boat ride feels like?

Dad looks into Mom's eyes, then Henry's. He can only sigh and ready the boat.

Mom parks herself in the passenger seat. "We don't have to go far."

"I assure you, we won't."

Dad, Henry, and I pile in. Naturally, I forget the life jacket, so I pin Henry against my legs and keep a sharp lookout for ducks.

While Dad putt-putts around the cove, Henry's nose goes into overdrive. His gaze darts in circles, and his ears twitch forward and backward until they about flip inside out. At least he stays put, albeit sitting with his nose in the air like some regal prince of the high seas.

I repeat—he's not a normal dog.

Then comes the inevitable. We run into someone we know.

I'd rather wave and scoot on by, but my dad's a talker. I mean that in a good way. He's friendly and tells a great story. Consequently, he knows all thirty thousand people who live at the lake.

It doesn't come as any great surprise when he stops the boat and chats with a guy on a dock. When they run out of small talk, the man says, "You out fishing?"

My dad shrugs. "Oh, no. Just . . . out . . ."

The man's brow puckers. "Oh?"

I understand his confusion. I mean, when it comes to boats, you can fish, cruise, or sunbathe. We clearly aren't sharing a picnic basket in the sunshine, and we admitted to not fishing. But when you're cruising in your boat, you generally go more than a hundred feet. Certainly farther than you can see from your own dock.

My dad coughs. Great. He's going to fess up.

"Uh," he drawls, "we're just taking the dog for a ride."

The man lets that sink in for a moment. Then he frowns as if he still doesn't get it. "You're taking your dog for a boat ride?"

Dad chuckles. "Yeah."

The man blinks at us.

We look back at him as if we're normal. I don't think he buys it. "Well . . . have fun then."

Right. We wave and toodle straight back home, lest we run across anyone else my dad knows.

Henry's face falls when we pull into our dock, and he gives us that "Oh, can't we do it again?" look.

I cross my arms. "Not happening, Henry."

Then again, you never know. Because later that week I see the neighbor and his two corgis down on his dock. The man carries a doggie life jacket.

My jaw about hits my knees. "Henry, look! A doggie jacket. You're not alone."

Those dogs are always on the dock, and I've never once seen them wear a life jacket, let alone fall in.

The neighbor buckles one dog into the life jacket, lowers his wave runner, hops on, and calls to the dog.

The dog vaults onto the seat behind him. The wave runner roars to life, and they take off across the lake.

And I felt stupid for taking Henry on a boat ride, why?

That little dog looks like he's having a jolly time aboard the wave runner. Of course, I'd never dream of doing that with Henry. He'd want to drive (he's stubborn that way), and we'd probably get a ticket for running down ducks.

Five minutes later, the neighbor returns, docks his wave runner, and takes the life jacket off dog one. Then dog two wiggles into the thing, hops aboard, and off they go.

Henry watches their wake as they trail out the cove. He wrinkles his forehead and gives me that sad-eyed puppy look.

I picture myself with a big honkin' dog clambering onto a seat way too small and careening our way around the lake.

It could only end in an embarrassing encounter with the water patrol.

In the distance, the neighbor's wave runner sputters back into the cove. Henry cocks his head and turns to me once again.

I meet his gaze. "That's for little dogs, Henry. You're not a little dog."

He stares at me as if my words have no meaning, which I suppose they don't. Somehow that never stops me from trying to reason with him.

"You're not a well-trained dog, either. That's not for amateurs, ya know."

Gaze. Gaze. Gaze.

"Henry, I promise, you'll fall in the water . . ."

Gaze.

"Dunkaroo . . ."

This dog could win a staring contest with a marble statue. How does he manage to make me feel so guilty?

Reasoning time over. I stand up and tug his leash. "Henry, let's go inside and get a *bone*."

He perks an ear, cocks his head, and gives me the *yeahyeahyeah* look.

Sure, *now* he understands every word. You know what I think? My ridiculous dog is a genius manipulator.

11

I keep thinking if we can just make it past the two-year mark, Henry will lose some of his exuberance and settle down.

Wrong. He's like a wind-up toy that never, ever stops.

After the epic fail of the scooter plan, I devise a new wear-out-the-dog strategy. This one involves my bicycle. For a moment I get that Wile E. Coyote feeling, like I'm moving from one Acme disaster to another. I dismiss it, though, because what's life without hope?

This time I figure to coast on my bike while Henry trots alongside. After all, I'm more proficient on my bike than on some wobbly, electric, death mobile. For one thing, there won't be any engine to scare Henry, and for another, I've logged enough bike miles that I can easily ride one-handed, holding the leash in my left hand where Henry's used to traveling. No tying anything to the handlebars.

I put my plan into action the next morning at dawn, while it's too early for witnesses.

Henry loves walks, so I ease his leash off its peg. I don't need to start out my experiment with a delirious dog. Before I can summon him with a let's-go-for-a-walk whisper, he leaps from his prone position to a flat-out run straight at me, a few midair twists of joy thrown in for fun.

So much for calm.

I wrangle the collar on Henry's leaping, dancing body and head out the door before he wrenches my arm from the socket. Then I let him hop around the front yard and piddle on all the grass, trees, bushes, and flowers he can. Once we start the ride, I don't want him making a beeline for every mailbox and hydrant.

When he's run dry, I head for the garage. "Okay, Henry. Time for some exercise."

My bike helmet hangs on a nail, and at first I don't grab it. I'm only going to coast around.

Visions of Death by Scooter Ride swamp me. I yank the helmet down and secure it to my head.

As we cross the garage toward the bike rack, Henry gives the scooter a wide berth. I've probably afflicted him with a lifelong paranoia. How's he going to feel about my bike? I've not had it out when he's been near. Will he view it as another freak of nature?

With trepidation, I pull my mountain bike off the rack. Henry springs forward with a "This must be a new toy" bounce. He sniffs the wheels, the chain, the pedals, and finally the frame. Then he looks up at me, his mouth grinning in anticipation of some excellent game.

I should probably be leery of this latest bipolar manifestation. Instead, a little bubble of hope forms in my chest. "You're not scared of it?"

He wags his stub of a tail.

I wheel the bike down the driveway, and Henry trots alongside. Then he rears up on his hind legs and, in classic boxer play, swipes a paw at the front tire.

I jerk to a stop. "Henry, no! You'll get your paw caught in the spokes."

Henry cocks his head and gives me a look that says, "Yippee, let's play."

"It's not a toy. We're going to exercise."

I ease down the driveway, but two steps later he tries to bat the tire again.

"Knock it off!"

Only my dog would think boxing with a moving bike is an exciting plan. I wait longer before trying again. With stop-and-go progress, we blunder down the driveway.

At the street, I have one final this-might-be-a-bad-idea moment, but I dismiss it. Surely Henry will forget about boxing once he gets moving. I'm desperate to exercise him. I'll stick my arm way out to keep him away from the tires . . .

I launch the bike.

Henry shifts immediately out of play mode and into a thousand-yard sprint, but I'm ready for him. He doesn't get two steps before I hit my rear brake and hop off the bike.

"Henry, we're going to trot."

He dances like he can't wait to run free, then stops and boxes at the tire, tangling his feet in the leash. Now I have to unsnarl the mess.

My shiny bike has no kickstand, and I don't want to lay it on the street, so I hold the bike up with one hand. With the other hand, I attack Henry's jumble.

He thinks I've joined the boxing match and rakes a claw down my arm.

"Ow! Quit it, Henry."

I stick one foot out trying to keep him at bay, which leaves me hopping on the other foot while I disentangle the leash. Somehow I still keep my bike from toppling. I don't know how.

I pin Henry in an I-hate-you-right-now glare. "Let's try again."

I kick off the curb, and this time Henry's body swings into an easy lope. His speed meshes with my bike's casual coast, and for all of thirty paces I'm a dog-training genius. A breeze fans through the vents on my helmet and teases a grin to my face, even if I do look stupid leaning over with my arm straight out to keep a dog leash away from the bike.

Henry catches the frolic in my mood. He angles sharply toward the front tire, stops, and rears up to wrestle it.

"Nooo!" I screech the brake and jump off again. My heart stampedes in the post-panic of barely averted disaster. Henry's missed the tire, at least. Mostly because he's got terrible aim.

Six or seven deep breaths and a few mutterings of "What are you thinking, you dingbat dog?" eventually calm me. Henry dances at my side like he can't decide whether tearing across the neighborhood or play-fighting my bike is a more splendid use of this delicious summer morning.

Now what? Scratch the plan? For a few moments it had almost kinda sorta worked.

Is there any other way? I filter my options.

I have rollerblades.

Right. Put on something with no brakes whatsoever and let Henry tow me to China.

Perhaps I need to move a little faster on the bike so he focuses on running and forgets about playing.

It could work.

Maybe.

A construction truck lumbers toward the intersection three houses down. Henry's posture stiffens to alert, but the vehicle rumbles off in the opposite direction.

It's worker time already? I'd floundered longer than I thought. Henry doesn't approve of noisy construction. I need a hurry-up offense if I'm going to score on this exercise deal before the neighborhood comes alive with hammers, saws, and cement trucks.

I turn my bike toward the nearest cul-de-sac—one that has no houses under construction.

"All right, Henry, let's run."

This time I shove off hard downhill and Henry is running from step one. We sail into the cul-de-sac, and there's a teensy problem. I'm out of road, but Henry doesn't care. I sense his body beelining for the high curb, the grass, and a six-foot fence beyond. I offer a quick prayer to the God who still loves me even when I'm shortsighted.

Somehow, with an off-balance tug on the leash—and probably a whopping load of divine intervention—I force Henry to follow the curve of the cul-de-sac. Round and round we go.

I don't know how to straighten him out, but I'm okay with that. No one can bother us here.

We go another five minutes on the spin cycle.

He's running, he's foaming at the mouth, all is well.

Except there's only so many times I can ride in a circle before I misplace my mind.

Eight more laps and I'm ready to kill something, even if it's me. I give another tug at the leash. The bike straightens and heads up the road.

Wonder of wonders, Henry gallops right alongside me. We zoom past houses and driveways. No leaping, no boxing. I'd scream with delight except I don't want to shatter Henry's "I will run nicely by my mommy" mood. I don't even care that we still look dumb.

Soon we pass a parked cement truck, then an open-doored trailer full of house-framing tools. We're going farther than I planned, but this is SO working.

Six houses later an entire roof crew rains laughter on me and shouts odd phrases in Spanish, of which I only catch *el perro*—dog. I hope they mean Henry.

At least no one is in the street to distract Henry.

Scratch that. I see one guy in the distance. He shoots a power washer at a bunch of dirt on the right side of the road. I maneuver to the far left.

As we glide closer, the noise of the washer assaults my ears. I peek at Henry. His focus is all run, like nothing else in the world matters.

Three strides later, Henry's head shoots upward like he's just spotted a threat, and nothing else in the world matters except the evil, noisy hose.

Henry's body morphs into a lion on the hunt—no, on the chase. He shoots ahead, cuts right, and flashes in front of my bike.

Suddenly I'm airborne like a sick, lopsided bird, and I'm treated to a sky view of my bike crumpling into the pavement. As it burns into my memory, I realize what a bad, bad plan this was. I'm still attached to the dog, I'm not wearing body armor—not even a padded bra—and I'm about to go the way of the bike.

Crunch.

Everything hurts, so apparently I'm not dead. My arm—the one attached to Henry's leash—whips around as I try to uncrumple the rest of my limbs. At least Henry isn't towing me anywhere.

I glance up to see Power-Washer Guy staring at me, his mouth agape. He still holds the hose aimed who knows where. His eyes don't laugh. Instead, I read sympathy. He takes a step toward me as if to help me up.

Henry gives the full show of defense—raised hackles and raucous barking—because the evil hose just might kill us all.

The man's eyes pop wide, and his hands—hose and all—fly up as if he were under arrest. Somehow his forward step takes him three feet backward, and his face freezes in a panicked look that says, "Sorry, lady, you're on your own."

For the sake of Power-Washer Guy, I struggle to my knees. I can't find enough breath in my lungs to reprimand Henry, but I know getting the bike up will divert his attention.

My elbows feel raw, my legs like Silly Putty. The rest of me—surprise, surprise—hurts like I got wrenched over my handlebars and slammed into asphalt.

In a haze, I stand and somehow force the bike upright too. Henry turns from Power-Washer Guy and skips to my side for a reunion with his dearest friend in the world—my torn-up bike. Is the thing even going to roll anymore?

I don't bother assessing; I just shove it toward home. As I limp along, I recite a new self-preservation principle: never be on wheels when any part of my body is attached to a mentally disturbed dog.

Why do the obvious rules of physics elude me?

I figure I'll be long paying in pain for today's calamity, but to my surprise, I walk off most of my throbbing before I hit my doorstep. My bike seems to shake off its trauma as well, except for the scratches that will forever memorialize my human cannonball routine. If this is the worst of the ordeal, it feels like I've gotten off easily. I should be thankful.

But I'm not.

I didn't know I was signing up for this when we got Henry. I mean, it's not like our family went to a breeder and said, "Oh, please, give us a lunatic dog who's going to wreck our lives."

Yet here I am, on a train headed right down that track.

But what's the alternative? Dump Henry because he's a big, fat pain in the caboose? Is that what we want to teach our kids?

12

I wait for some further medical consequence of the bike fiasco, but nothing happens to me. After a few days of rain, an overload of kid activities, and a trip out of town for a family reunion, the whole incident evaporates from my mind.

It feels like forever since I've slipped away for my own exercise (aka sanity maintenance—Henry's not allowed to come). My favorite workout is a nine-mile bike ride around a nearby lake. I'm about twitching to feel the wind through my helmet vents, so the next morning I bulldoze through the house, willing to mow down any dog, kid, or husband who stands between me and my bike. The attitude is unnecessary—they're all still asleep.

I'm happily pedaling into the wind, breathing in the sunrise, when I start to have chest pains.

I don't suffer from perpetual brilliance—you'll have picked that up by now—so it's understandable why I simply keep riding. They aren't bad pains.

Yeah, probably the last words of a lot of middle-aged adults.

I survive, though, and the next day I'm riding again. This time I don't even make it one-fourth of the way around before I'm hurting. But it's probably not a heart attack. After all, I've never had a heart attack before, so I'm likely not having one now. Stunning logic, I know.

In one of those moments where I make Malibu Barbie look like a rocket scientist, I decide to keep pedaling rather than turn around. Halfway through the circuit, my denial loses its appeal. It's pretty lonely on the backside of that trail if you don't count the guy I call Cigar Man. And I don't count him because anyone who walks an exercise trail while puffing a cigar is probably not there for the exercise. I wouldn't want to fall unconscious around him. Normally I don't worry, because there's no way Cigar Man could catch me on my bike. But me being slumped over having a heart attack just might give him the edge.

It seems prudent to stop and rest before Cigar Man comes along. I'm sure Barbie would agree. After a minute or two my heart rate is down and the pain is better. Time to get moving. I take a deep cleansing breath, only I never get to the cleansing part because I've suddenly discovered the meaning of "stabbing pain." Frightening, but also a clue. It shouldn't be a heart attack if a deep breath set it off.

In a weird sort of way, that makes me feel better. I can just take shallow breaths for the next few miles and everything will be fine. I set off to brave Cigar Man on the back forty.

Shallow breaths turn out to be highly unrealistic, but I'm a long way from home so I ride through the pain—grumbling, grimacing, and looking every bit the wild-eyed, muttering maniac. That'll teach Cigar Man to glance my way. Of course, I do meet a few normal people. They look at me like I'm Cigar Man.

I finally make it safely home. Do you think the first thing I do is call my doctor? No siree. It only hurts when I exercise, and I'm done exercising for today.

Instead, I start on my interminable to-do list. Oh, joy. Vacuuming.

I drag out the Hoover, shove a brush attachment on the hose, and head for the kitchen. It's always depressing to count the new claw marks Henry's made on our cheap wood floor, so today I pretend I don't see them. By the time I haven't noticed the third one, my mysterious pain strikes again.

Now is an excellent time to call the doctor. Then I won't have to vacuum. Or count claw marks.

It's funny how quickly you can get an appointment when you mention chest pains. I don't even have time to take Henry for his better-behavior-through-exhaustion walk. (Yes, we're back to walks. No, they don't work. Yes, I'm still dumb enough to try.)

I'm fine with skipping our routine, since I feel like I swallowed a chainsaw. Soon I'm sitting in an exam room, and my doctor bustles in.

"Hi, Elaine," he says in a pleasant, friendly voice.

I don't feel pleasant and friendly back, though, because my name isn't, and never has been, Elaine.

He figures that out and moves on. No apology, just some paltry excuse about having seen it on someone else's chart. Don't doctors read the chart on the door before they see the patient? What if the wrong chart was on my door?

To head off any confusion, I start right in about my chest pain. Then the nurse hands me a flimsy paper vest—circus-tent size.

She and the doctor step out. Pointless, really, because the armholes gape to my waist. So much for preserving my modesty. Does the paper vest company really only make one size?

When the doctor comes back, he listens to my heart. Then he examines my rib cage.

"Tell me if this hurts." He presses on my ribs.

I'm suddenly three feet above the table, clawing the air. I forget to tell him it hurts, but he gets the idea.

"Have you been in a car accident?"

In the midst of pain fog, I struggle to review my recent driving record. "Um, no . . ."

"You play sports? Maybe you took a ball to the chest or collided with someone?"

Sports . . . a ball . . .

Football fades in, but I haven't caught a touchdown pass in years. Soccer's even more distant. "Um, no . . ."

"Hmm." He prods a bit more.

I try to keep from leaping to the moon.

Finally he says I'm not having a heart attack. Good news.

But I have something called blah-blah-itis. I've never heard of it. This doctor has a habit of using six-syllable words that all sound alike no matter how many times he repeats them.

He also tells me I need a blood test to investigate the cause of my tachy-blah-blah. Apparently, I have tachy-blah-blah *and* blah-blah-itis. Oh, fortunate me. Furthermore, I'm getting a bunch of tests with initials in them to confirm the diagnosis.

Then he asks how I sleep at night.

"Very badly. We've talked about this before. You've written me several prescriptions, which aren't helping."

He frowns and looks at my chart. I guess Elaine sleeps like a rock.

"Well, you need sleep so your body gets a chance to heal. Have you ever tried Oxa-blah-blah? That works like blah-blah but doesn't blah. Or you could try blah-blah, but Lunesta blah blah blah . . ."

He lost me after the first blah-blah.

Then his cell phone rings and he answers it. Maybe Elaine wouldn't mind, but I do. I'm the one in the paper towel.

While he chatters with his phone friend, the nurse says to me, "So, do you want the prescription for Oxa-blah-blah?"

"Which drug was that exactly? The one that works like Lunesta, or the antihistamine, or something else I didn't understand?"

"I don't know. I wasn't listening."

This alarms me enough to consider a mad dash from the office, but it's just plain awkward to juke a nurse and sprint through the lobby while dressed in a gaping paper vest.

The doctor ends his call, and the nurse turns to him. "Is Oxa-blah-blah the one that works like Lunesta?"

He gives her a look that clearly says, "A nurse should know that."

Somehow she doesn't catch the look. "I wasn't paying attention to your discussion."

Now his look says, "Remind me why I hired you?"

She doesn't catch that either. Here's hoping she has a second career in mind.

I keep my mouth shut and think maybe it wouldn't be all that disturbing to run screaming from the building. Would they still charge me for the visit?

The doctor writes a prescription for Oxa-blah-blah, tells the nurse to schedule my tests, and heads out the door. Poor Elaine is probably still waiting somewhere.

The nurse wants to schedule fasting blood work for the following morning.

Major trauma.

Not the needle. The fasting. Skipping breakfast is my worst thing ever. It scandalizes my must-eat-every-two-hours metabolism. If not for love of my bike ride, I would never agree to this.

I also need a stress test, which requires intelligent insurance planning. All tests and lab work done at the doctor's office on the same day are covered by the same co-payment. I save thirty dollars scheduling the stress test the same day as the blood work.

Saving money is almost as important to me as breakfast.

There's no way I want to go traipsing on a treadmill before I've eaten. If I faint on the thing, we'd never know the cause of my tachy-blah-blah. So we schedule the test for a couple of hours after the blood work. That way I have time to eat.

The next morning, my stomach threatens to cave in on itself. I have to feed the dog before I leave for my blood test, and the kibble almost smells good.

I'm no happier when I arrive at the doctor's office. My blood vessels shrivel up when I'm cold, and the temperature feels like it's been set by a pack of menopausal women.

The lab tech ties up my arm, gives me a ball to squeeze, cleans a semi-promising area, and jabs in the needle.

No blood comes out.

So what does she do? She starts digging around.

They always do that. They can't just take the needle out and try again. That would be admitting they missed. Instead they grope under your skin, jabbing willy-nilly into your muscle tissue as if that didn't count for about sixty-five different misses.

Finally I've had enough of blind man's bluff. I scoot forward in the chair like I'm considering a counterattack. "This isn't working. Maybe I've got inferior veins or something. They disappear when I get cold. What if I go outside and warm up?"

Soon I'm standing outside the doctor's office waiting for my veins to come back.

And waiting.

Did I mention that I didn't get any breakfast?

I start flapping my arms. Hunger makes me do dumb things.

No veins.

What now? Jumping jacks? That'll be great for my tachy-blah-blah.

Instead, I stand there soaking up the sun. I'll probably get melanoma. Who would deal with our nutcase dog all day if that happened? Eventually I see a squiggly vessel or two, so I trot back inside. By the time I get to the lab, shrivel city. The tech decides to try the other arm. She ties it off, cleans it up, jabs it.

No blood.

The digging starts.

I grit my teeth. "That hurts."

"I don't want to have to stick you again."

Because incessantly stabbing my muscle tissue is better?

By this time, another tech has come along. They consult and then try the first arm again.

Strike three.

Now the first tech is really rattled, so the second gal takes over. She's the one who does the tough sticks. Where was she three strikes ago?

Miss Tough Stick gives the second arm another go. She ties it. She cleans it. She jabs it.

No blood.

This is getting serious. My stress test looms, and I need food.

"I could write you a script and you could get your blood drawn somewhere else," the first tech says, clearly hoping I'll go away forever.

I'll bet most people would have been smart enough to do just that, but not me. I'd have to fast again. And pay more money.

I'm not moving until they get my blood.

Miss Tough Stick isn't ready to give up either. Both arms are wasted, so she checks out the back of my hand. There's another discussion about needle sizes, tubes, and veins. Finally they tie it, clean it, jab it.

Zippo.

If it didn't defy all the known realm of science, these two ladies would swear I didn't have a drop of blood in my body.

"I could write you a script and you could get your blood drawn somewhere else," the first tech repeats.

The second tech decides to call in the big guns. She goes for the doctor.

"I don't remember the last time he stuck anyone," the first tech says to me.

I sink lower in my chair and gulp my unsatisfying breakfast substitute—otherwise known as water.

The doctor breezes in and looks me over, tsk-tsk-tsking about all the bruises and Band-Aids.

"So when's the last time you did this?" I say.

"Relax. I used to be the blah-blah-blah-ist over at blah-blah."

Oh. No worries then.

The doctor decides he's going to show these techs a thing or two, and starts blah-blah-ing about how to do this right. He's got the back of my other hand.

He ties, cleans, jabs.

Glory be! Some blood comes out.

Then stops.

The smug look slides off his face. He starts digging.

"Oww!"

"I'm in. I know I'm in. Are you dehydrated?"

I wave my does-nothing-for-my-empty-belly water. "I've been drinking."

"Your perfusion is terrible. You're dehydrated." He pulls the needle out and turns to the techs. "I want a urinalysis done. We have to test her blah-blah blah-der function." Then back to me, "You're dehydrated. Come back another day—in the afternoon—when you're fully hydrated."

He marches out the door.

Six stabs, no blood, and apparently it's all my fault.

"I could write you a script and you could get your blood drawn somewhere else," the first tech says.

You'd think I'd walk out the door and never come back.

But what if I really am dehydrated? And what about my stress test? Maybe I should drink more, and then have them take my blood after the stress test. If they don't get my blood today, I'll have to fork over another thirty-dollar co-pay.

Sure. Hook me up to a bunch of wires and put me on a treadmill moving at high speeds when I'm ready to faint from hunger. (It sounded plausible at the time.)

So I drink a lot of water. A whole lot.

I mean LOTS and LOTS.

The nurse calls me for the test, and I joke about how much water I've been drinking.

"Do you need to use the restroom?" she says.

"I just did." A tidal wave, really. My poor bladder didn't know what hit it.

"Do you want to go again? It takes a while to get the wires connected for your test. Once we start, you can't leave the room."

"I should be okay."

What she didn't tell me was that I'd have to stand around forever while she sandpapered various spots on my body. Then she'd stick on suction cups, test them, and sandpaper some more. In addition to failed blood stick Band-Aids, I'm now covered with red sandpapered spots.

Finally, we're ready to start the test. I'm a bit intimidated by all the wires, and I begin to wonder if this is dangerous. After all, we're testing my heart here. I only have one. Do these people know CPR? More important, can they do it better than they can draw blood?

Keeling over and leaving my hubby to raise our boys alone is one thing, but throwing a maniac dog into the deal is asking too much.

Turns out that Doctor Blah-blah isn't even present for the test. Instead I get a physician's assistant. Not a nurse, not a doctor, but she can write prescriptions. Sounds fishy, but I've got twenty-five wires suctioned to my body. I should have questioned this a lot earlier.

"Okay, start the treadmill," says Doctor Substitute.

"I guess now's a bad time to say I need to pee."

They laugh, but I'm not kidding. "How long is the test?"

"About ten minutes," says Nurse Sandpaper.

Next thing I know, I'm staggering and panting up a steep, slippery slope, while my eyeballs nearly pop out from heinous bladder abuse.

Ten minutes can be a very long time.

When the test is through, they have to peel off all the suction cups before I can leave.

"Just rip them off." I cross my legs lest I release Niagara Falls. "It can't hurt any worse than all those needles."

Doctor Substitute gives me a puzzled look, so I zip through the story.

"I can draw your blood," she says.

Why not? Everyone else has tried it.

I look at my veins. They're popping out, much like my eyeballs, but for veins it's a good thing. Maybe I can finally get this done and get home. Who knows what evil Henry is perpetrating in my absence. "Can I use the restroom first?"

"Sure."

By the time I get back to Doctor Substitute, my veins have disappeared.

"Hmm." She looks over my assortment of misses. "We'll try your ankle. If that doesn't work, we can always use the jugular."

I hope she's kidding.

She takes my right ankle, ties it, cleans it, jabs it.

Doctor Substitute gets no blood. Not even close. She gives up on the ankle.

"Hmm." She inspects my neck.

Yikes. She was serious about the jugular.

"You have a very nice vein here. I can see it throbbing."

I'm an exhausted, half-starved, bladder-maimed pincushion, so I don't remember that it's arteries that throb. Arteries—as in those things that spurt blood across the room if you sever them.

"I'm sure I can hit it," says Doctor Substitute. "Want me to try?"

"Um, okay."

She jabs.

"Did you get it?"

I feel another jab.

"Now did you get it?"

"No."

Aim your Band-Aid at my backside, honey. I'm leavin'.

I spend the weekend suffering bike withdrawal and wrestling with my ridiculous problem. I can't ride without the results of my blood work, but there's no blood for said work.

Henry spends the weekend whining for me to walk him, which I'm not supposed to do. I'm probably not supposed to be chasing him through the house, trying to retrieve a pair of stolen underwear either, but some things are nonnegotiable.

The quickest way to silence the dog—not to mention getting me back to the refuge of my bike ride—is through my doctor's office so they can do the labs right away.

Assuming they manage to get blood.

Maybe I really was dehydrated, 'cause I find it hard to believe that missing nine times is possible under normal conditions. I mean, whoever heard of such a thing?

Monday morning I return to the dreaded office. Every pore of my body oozes breakfast-withdrawal crabbiness. But at least no one can accuse me of dehydration. I sucked in more water than an entire football team on two-a-day practices. You haven't lived until you've spent your whole weekend gulping and urinating.

I see the first tech in the hallway. Her eyes go wide and she runs away.

A different tech arrives and starts the routine—the vein search, the tie, the swab, yada, yada, yada.

She aims and jabs.

Total miss.

I don't need a repeat performance of last week, so I speak right up.

"Why don't you just go get a doctor?"

Wouldn't you know it? She retrieves Doctor Blah-blah. He halts midswagger when his eyes meet mine. Do I see a bead of sweat forming? This is almost entertaining. Almost.

He takes his best shot.

Zilcho.

I am the bloodless wonder.

"I could write you a script and you could get your blood drawn somewhere else," the tech says.

Maybe now is the time to listen to that little voice inside my head. The one that's been saying, "Run, you idiot."

So I run. Right to the blood draw station at the hospital.

This presents a whole new set of issues. For one thing, my arms and hands are covered with bruises that would put your standard junkie to shame. The hospital tech's eyebrows hike up when he sees my array of black and blue.

Hmm, tell him the story or let him think I'm an addict? Is he really going to understand that missing my bike ride interferes with logical reasoning? That I was dumb enough to let someone repeatedly puncture my body with a sharp object?

"Uh, they missed . . . a lot . . . and sent me here."

I avoid looking him in the eye, because I don't really want to read "simpleton" in his gaze. Thankfully, he gets down to business.

Within three and a half seconds, he's surveyed both arms, wrapped a rubber tube around my left forearm, and swiped me with alcohol.

I have a scant two seconds to realize he means to stick me in my lower, inner arm, and while I do see a vein there, it looks pretty deep so it's probably going to—

OUCH.

Before I can ask if this guy knows what he's doing, I see my ruby red blood coursing into the tube.

He pops a full tube off, fills another, and is bandaging my arm before I can get my mouth closed. I didn't even have time to get comfortable in the chair.

Next thing I know, he hands over my paperwork and ushers me out the door. If I didn't have a brand new Band-Aid on my arm, I'd think the whole episode was just a hunger-induced fantasy.

Then I see the bill.

One needle jab, one minute of labor, $225.

Really?

Worse, I've come to a hospital, so my insurance will apply that to my deductible. In other words, I've gotta pay the whole wad.

Two days later, my doctor's office calls.

"Your blood work came back normal," the nurse says.

"That's great." Assuming it's actually my blood and not Elaine's. "What about everything else?"

"All fine. Your tachy-blah-blah isn't dangerous, but if you want, the doctor will give you a prescription of Meto-blah that might help."

"Meto-what?"

"It's a blood pressure medication."

"I need blood pressure medication?"

"Well, no. Just if you want it."

My eyebrows pinch together with the start of a headache. "Isn't my blood pressure nearly too low as it is?"

"Then you don't want it?"

"Why in the world did the doctor suggest it?"

"I'll check." There's silence for a while, then she comes back on the line. "Apparently, it lowers your heart rate too. Like a side effect."

"So I'd be taking a medication I don't need, just for a side effect?"

More silence.

"Let's scratch that plan. What can I do about the chest pain?"

"Nothing but rest and Motrin or Advil."

Great. No three-syllable, unpronounceable wonder drug for that. "How long?"

"At least a week. Maybe two. Possibly three or—"

"Yeah, I get the idea. Thanks."

How am I going to keep myself from suffering exercise withdrawal for this indeterminate amount of time?

Two weeks later, I realize exercise withdrawal is only half my torment. The other half is Henry's exercise withdrawal. Not that the rest of the family doesn't pitch in with him. But between all their activities, they simply don't have the kind of time required to induce tranquility in a wrecking ball of a dog.

Yes, I know. He's a stinky pain. But he's *our* stinky pain, and I can't help feeling sorry for him. If only there were an easier way to get him the exercise he needs. Maybe I should try the electric scooter again?

Um, no. Been there, nearly crashed that.

Maybe coasting on my bike? Um, no. That was a disast—

And that's when realization jabs me like a needle in the backside.

I suppose I should have dredged this out of my repressed memory earlier. I'm sure I would have if the doctor had been more specific in his questioning about accidents.

Like if instead of asking about car collisions or a penalty kick to the chest, he'd said, "What about a bike trauma? Any chance your whacko dog darted after a power washer and catapulted you over your handlebars?"

That would've at least cleared up the origin of my pain. Ah, but would I have wanted to admit to that fiasco?

People say dogs are expensive—the food, the vet bills, the occasional chewed-up shoe.

Right. Thanks to Henry, I've got twelve needle punctures, an inflamed rib cage, a nice bill from the hospital, and a questionable grip on what's left of my self-respect.

Would it kill that dog to give me a Lassie moment?

Just one?

13

Unlikely as it seems, Henry graduates his second obedience course, and even makes it through the third class. We discover he can be extremely obedient.

When he wants to.

He doesn't always want to. And when obedience doesn't strike his fancy, Jekyll turns to Hyde.

Once we finish classes, we lose the routine of daily training. Henry becomes more and more demanding. If he wants to play, and you don't, too bad for you. He brings his toy to your lap and chews on the thing. We can't find a "go away" command he'll agree to. If we block him from getting to us, then he barks.

And barks.

And barks.

How do you get a barking dog to stop? If we yell, he barks louder. Believe me, he has an obnoxious set of pipes.

If we try to approach him, turbo-dog springs into action. Ah, the thrill of the chase. Jumping, twisting, dodging, sprinting, *and* barking.

I mentioned the barking?

Probably good we don't own a gun.

We try to extinguish the behavior by turning our back and ignoring him. He has a game plan for that. It's called, Bite the Behind.

Man, that dog is fast.

He keeps his mouth soft—he's not trying to hurt us. It's a play bite to get our attention. If we whirl around to keep our backside safe, he scampers momentarily away only to turn, dash at our hands, and grab at them.

And if we put our hands behind our back? Er, how shall I say this nicely? For Alan and the boys, hands behind their back while facing the dog is particularly dangerous, as Henry lacks discretion over which dangling body part he'll nip.

Not that he bites hard.

Right. No consolation there.

I reach the end of my tolerance one day at the dog park. Henry decides he'd rather play with me than with all the other dogs there. I suppose I should be flattered, but his idea of playing together means we run around nipping, wagging, drooling, and chasing.

"Henry, look at all these fine, four-legged creatures. Surely one of them would like to chase you."

He stands, his back stiff with resolution, and gives me his answer: BarkBarkBarkBarkBarkBarkBarkBarkBarkBarkBarkBarkBark.

I park my hands on my hips. "I brought you here to socialize with other dogs. You see me every day."

BarkBarkBarkBarkBarkBarkBarkBarkBarkBarkBarkBark.

"You think you're going to get your way by being obnoxious?"

BarkBarkBarkBarkBarkBarkBarkBarkBarkBarkBarkBark.

Thankfully, another lady and her dog approach. The little pooch sniffs at Henry and distracts him.

The lady smiles. "Hi. That your dog?"

"Yeah. Henry."

"He's beautiful."

"Thanks. What kind of dog is yours?"

"Oh, just a mix. But he's a good boy." At which point, her dog trots to her, cuddles for a moment or two, then dashes off to play.

Henry doesn't follow.

I wave him away. "Go play with your new friend."

BarkBarkBarkBarkBarkBarkBarkBarkBarkBarkBarkBark.

The woman blinks.

"Henry, I'm not going to play with you now."

Henry moves to Plan B. "B" for Bad Doggie. He dashes at my hands and tries to grab them.

The lady takes a big step backward.

Henry ramps up his theatrics, adding growling for dramatic effect.

The lady's mouth hangs open. "Oh my! What's this behavior?"

Aside from an Oscar-worthy performance? "That's just Henry trying to make me play with him."

He dashes at me, snatches my hand, releases it, and scampers out of reach.

BarkBarkBarkBa—

"*No*, Henry!"

This show is getting ridiculous. I need my own Plan B for Bad Doggie, but what can I do? He's not on the leash, so I can't yank it. With a stiff twist of my shoulders, I turn away from him.

He goes for my rear end.

The lady takes another step back. "Does he do this a lot?"

"Yeah." My brain scans for options. Can I catch him?

The park is only nine thousand square yards. I'll just hop into my supersonic jumpsuit.

I can't discipline him, I can't catch him, and I can't ignore him. What's left?

"I guess I better go now."

I wheel around and head for the gate. The one with the big sign that says "Aggressive Behavior Strictly Prohibited."

Henry follows. I knew he would. He'd made up his mind that I would play with him, and if there's such a thing as a Doggie Code of Conduct, Henry's favorite command would read "Thou shalt not derail thy one-track mind."

We create a charming parade. I lead. Henry trails—dashing, barking, and nipping at my rear end.

I'm getting used to the whole spectacle thing.

One problem (okay, many, but for the moment, one). I still need to get Henry's leash on him.

He follows me into the enclosure of the park's double-gated entrance/exit, but then I have to corner him, which usually looks something like a greased pig contest at a county fair. Today I catch an amazing break—another dog wanders by and distracts him.

I snap the leash on Henry and walk him to the car, lecturing under my breath, while he skips with clueless joy. I hate that.

When I get home, I dial K9 University.

"Hi, this is Erin Young. We have a boxer named Henry—"

"Henn-ryyy! How's he doing?"

"That's why I called. He's acting up when he wants to play and we don't."

"What does he do?"

"Well, he barks and barks, and if we try to discipline him, he runs away, and we can't catch him until he's forgotten why we're after him."

"I see."

"And if we try to ignore him, he starts play-biting us. You can't even turn your back. He'll bite your behind."

Bless her heart, she doesn't laugh. Much. "What other behavior is he doing?"

"Now that you mention it, he's getting upset when he sees bike riders, dogs, squirrels—you name it—out the window. He jumps against it, and if I try to shoo him away, he barks and even nips at me."

"Oh, no!"

"Not viciously. I mean, he doesn't sink his teeth into me or anything. It's like he's so frustrated he doesn't know what to do."

"Sounds like you need a house call."

I blow out a huge sigh. "That would be great! Thank you so much."

We set it up, and a couple of days later I tell Jacob, "Angel's coming over today."

"Really? Why?"

"Well, you know how Henry's been behaving badly lately? Angel is going to help us deal with that."

"Great. Just make sure Henry greets him outside."

"Huh?"

Jacob looks at me like I'm fryin' the bacon with no flame. "Hello? It's Angel. What does Henry do every time he sees him?"

Ah.

Jacob nods. "Trust me, you want them outside."

Angel calls us when he reaches the neighborhood. "Hi, I'm here. Don't do anything unusual. I'm going to park and walk on the street in front of your house. I want to see Henry's reaction."

"Will do."

A car pulls up. The door opens. A strange man wearing a coat and glasses steps out. Henry shoots to the window, categorizes him as a class-one threat, and goes into barking, jumping, hyper-defense mode. Granted, Angel looks intimidating even to me, but whatever happened to being BFF with the whole blooming neighborhood?

Angel gets back in the car, drives away, and calls me again. "Was that his typical reaction?"

"Lately."

"Okay. We'll have to curb that. I'm going to park out of his view. Can you and Alan come outside to talk?"

"Sure."

Angel meets us sans coat and glasses. "How do you feel about using a shock collar?"

Funny he should mention it. Alan and I had talked about this very thing. It's not like we're eager to electrocute the dog, but we'd heard of people successfully using the collars for training.

With one glance, I read Alan's eyes. We both trust Angel.

"Let's give it a try." I actually feel some hope.

We sit outside while Angel explains how it works, taking care to show us how to use the minimum setting necessary.

He gives us a reassuring smile. "Think you got all that?"

Alan scans the buttons. "Looks simple enough."

Key words that always mean we won't do it right.

"Okay." Angel stands. "Let's go in and practice some situations."

I put a hand on his arm. "Do you mind if Henry greets you outside?"

He looks puzzled for only a second, then he laughs. "Not at all."

"I'll bring him out on the leash." Alan heads into the house.

"I really want to thank you for coming out here, Angel. I didn't know you made house calls."

"Oh, yeah. You have to see the dog in his environment."

"I'm worried about him."

"We'll get him through this. He's a great—"

The door bursts open and Henry, wriggling nose to tail, drags Alan straight for Angel. Nothing wrong with that dog's sniffer.

Angel spreads his arms wide. "Henn-ryyy!"

Wriggle, wriggle, fawn, fawn. Peeeeeeeee.

Clearly there's no escape from this charming ritual.

Henry, still thrilled out of his mind, jumps up on Angel.

"Off." He collars Henry and slips the electronic gizmo on him.

Henry neither notices nor cares because Angel is the love of his life. In delirium, he jumps again.

"Off!" This time Angel hits the zapper.

One tenth of a second at the lowest shock setting strikes Henry. He gives a tiny yelp and drops to all fours on the ground. His face registers total surprise.

Angel lets it sink in a moment, then calls a cheery, "Henn-ryyy!"

Henry wriggles with glee and trots to Angel, but doesn't jump. Angel thumps his chest in temptation for Henry to spring, but the dog's paws dance only on concrete.

My eyeballs about pop out. "It worked."

Angel nods. "Most dogs need a higher setting, but I always start with the lowest. Looks like that'll work for Henry. Let's try the window now."

We troop inside, and Angel gives us a quick review of the controls and exactly when to hit the button. Then he hands the thing to me. "Hide it behind your back so Henry doesn't realize you have anything. He'll simply hear your voice command and feel the twinge."

I nod, and Angel goes outside to don his evil intruder get-up.

I run through the sequence in my head: Wait until Henry reacts, but catch him before he jumps on the window. Press the momentary button—oops, which one is that? Oh yeah, it has a little bump so you can find it by feel. And what's that command again? I think we decided on "Phooey," a shortened German-ish phrase meaning, "You're being way too aggressive," but maybe it's supposed to be "Off" for jumping?

Before I sort it out, Angel strolls into the yard and Henry the Terrible runs howling for the window.

"Offooey!" I yell, brandishing my zapper and walloping the button.

Henry yelps and runs, tail tucked, to me. His nose finds the zapper, and his eyes give me an "Oooh, you got a scary new thing" look.

My gaze goes from Henry to my hand. Rats. I blew it on my first try. "I don't suppose I could convince you that my magical voice zapped you?"

Is it possible for a dog to roll his eyes?

We finish our session with Angel—I don't tell him I screwed up the hiding part—and settle in to a new life of promising obedience. Sort of.

"Henry, off!" *Zap.*

Works every time.

"Henry, off! Rats. Where's that stupid zapper? Off. Off. Henry, phooey! Who took the zapper?"

That one never works.

"Henry, off!" *Zap.* "Phooey!" *Zap.* "Phooey! Phooey!" *Zap, zap, zap.* "Hey, who took Henry's collar off?"

That one doesn't work either.

Angel figures we'll only need the collar for a few weeks, so he lets us borrow it. But sooner or later we have to give it back.

One day I stop by to see him. "I appreciate the collar loan, but we've had it for three weeks now. I think we're going to need to just buy one. You sell them here, don't you?"

"Yeah, but don't buy one. Hang on to ours a while longer."

"But Henry only behaves when he's wearing it. I think he's going to need one for the rest of his life."

"Give him some time. Stay consistent with your training. I'll call you when someone else needs it."

I have to smile on my way out the door. Angel's nice and all, but not much of a salesman. I appreciate that. I get the feeling he doesn't want any more shock collars in the world than are absolutely necessary.

A few weeks later, K9 University calls to say they need it back.

I take it to Angel the next day. "Thanks for letting us use this so long. I think we're going to need to buy one now."

"Don't do that yet. Let's see how Henry does. The people borrowing the collar only need it for a few days."

Is there something in my demeanor that says dog torturer? "Well, okay. We'll give it a go."

Three days later I'm back. "Henry has lost all fear of consequences. He's back to his tantrums at the window, and he won't listen to us."

Angel frowns. "Bad news. Turns out the other family needs my shock collar a few more days."

"Henry's had the collar routine figured from day one. If we could just put something on him that felt the same . . ."

"I have an old bark collar you could use. It doesn't work anymore, but it would feel like the shock collar when it's on his neck. Wanna try that?"

"You bet."

Two days later I'm back. "Henry understands the meaning of the word *placebo*."

Angel finally sells us a shock collar.

14

For $160, we buy some peace of mind—the collar cure-all. The thing is simpler and easier to operate than Angel's elaborate gizmo. Henry's barking tirades end, and I no longer have a bull's-eye on my behind.

Trouble is, the collar needs to be pretty tight to work properly. Two prongs stick out from a little box that fits snug to his neck. It has to be uncomfortable. I hate for Henry to wear it all day, so sometimes I leave it off when he gets up in the morning. He's always pretty good for the first few minutes he's awake.

After that, his mind gets stuck on *playwithmeplaywithmeplay withme*. As if I have nothing else to do? Like, say, getting the kids up, showered, breakfasted, and off to school on time?

It never takes long for him to roll out his bark-and-nip routine.

"Henry, please," I say pretty much every morning. "This is a stupid game."

BarkBarkBarkBarkBarkBarkBarkBarkBarkBarkBark.

"Why do we have to do this? I'm going to get the collar and put it on you so you'll be good. Surely you don't want to wear that thing all day?"

His response is always the same—the haunches up, shoulders down, "I love a good chase" pose.

So I snatch the collar and advance. "You know I'll catch you. I can move the coffee table and corner you. I'm smarter now."

This is his cue to spring straight into the air—backward. Voila. Sixty-five pounds of barking pogo-dog skip joyously through my house. On the bright side, this kind of racket gets my boys up before noon.

Every two days the collar lies charging in the laundry room at the other end of the house. I don't know why we think this location is a good idea. Without fail, pogo-dog bounces through the house after me, all the way to the collar. The moment my hand clasps it, the dance reverses.

Sometimes Alan's almost awake enough to help me catch Henry. One morning he hears the *barkbarkbark* routine and stomps toward us, collar in one hand, controller in the other. Bleary eyed, he presses a couple of buttons and listens for the test tone.

He frowns. "Is this thing working? Oww!"

Clunk.

I look at the collar on the floor. "It's working."

"You want to try it?"

"Not so much."

But I think we discovered a new method for waking a late riser.

As the months go by, an odd thing happens. The collar starts losing effectiveness. I know Henry has a high tolerance for discomfort, but to ignore the collar completely? We find ourselves setting the level higher.

Maybe its strength is weakening? I wait weeks, hoping for another accidental test from Alan.

Doesn't happen.

I eye the collar one day. Someone has to brave it.

I'm not the brave kind.

More months go by.

The collar might not impact Henry as much, but it still helps.

Even so, not all of his problems disappear. In the past, Charisma Dog turned on the charm and made instant pals of every household guest. Now he greets them with a sulky lack of hospitality.

I think the guitar lessons I started teaching in our home upset him—all that doorbell action going on while he's stuck in his crate, where he can't disrupt my students. They don't need his nose on their fretboard. It's not like he can help them find a C chord.

I try to have the boys walk Henry during lesson times, and that helps. But one day Jonathan and a new friend are goofing around in the house while I finish a guitar lesson. Just as I step out of the studio, Jacob brings Henry home. There's no warm fuzzy in Henry's greet-the-new-kid routine, so he earns an immediate trip to my bedroom for a doggie timeout.

I leave him there while I see my guitar student out, then I check on the boys. Meanwhile, Henry treats the whole household to whining. It sounds worse than anything my Van Halen wannabes could ever produce. When I go into my bedroom, Henry tries to shoot past me.

I block him and shut the door. "That's enough."

He barks, clearly agitated by the stranger in our house.

"He's a harmless kid."

Henry's gaze darts around the room, then he starts pacing like he's in some big cage. Every lap seems to frustrate him more.

I glare at him. "I'm not letting you out."

His gait edges toward manic, and he goes around a few more times. Then he falters and whines.

I cross my arms.

He kicks into another lap, but now there's more distress than confidence in his steps. It's like his circuits keep misfiring and he can't shut off his defend-or-die alarm.

As I watch him, my anger subsides. I see past his guard-dog overdrive to the unhappy dog underneath. Surely he doesn't want to be this way? A victim of whacked-out instincts he can't control?

I plunk to the floor. "Come here, Henry."

He prowls another lap or three before his body sags. Then he plops next to me.

I rub my hand along his soft coat.

He gives me a restless, sad-eyed look that says, "I don't know what to do with myself."

I do.

It's time for another visit with Angel.

I bring Henry along with me to K9 University. He loves visiting there. It smells like Angel.

I stop by a tree at the edge of the parking lot.

"Come on, Henry, let's do a precautionary piddle. Maybe you can greet Angel without watering him today."

Henry sniffs the tree, lifts his leg for all of half a second, then thinks the better of it.

I take him to the next elm over. "How 'bout a different tree? Surely this one needs your mark."

No dice.

"All right. Maybe you're empty."

We walk in and greet the gal at the desk. Angel is nowhere in sight—so much the better. Henry wanders on the end of his leash.

The gal leans against the counter. "How's Henry doing?"

"The shock collar seems—"

A splattering sound makes us both turn to Henry. His leg is lifted at their display table. A looping line of urine crisscrosses the decorative, hanging tablecloth.

"Henry!" I jerk his leash.

He glances up at me with an "I'm a little busy" look.

"Stop that!"

He calmly puts his leg down and waltzes my way. His eyes say, "All right, already. Can't a guy tinkle in peace?"

I turn to the front desk. "I'm really sorry. I tried to get him to go outside . . ."

Like that's believable given the soaked tablecloth? I shoot Henry a thanks-for-the-humiliation look.

He shakes his floppy ears and ignores me.

"No worries," the gal says. "So what's going on with the collar?"

"It seems to have less and less effect, and I'm worried Henry's getting more territorial."

While I fill her in on the details, her gaze washes over Henry. "Sounds like you need another house call. I'll check Angel's schedule and contact you."

"Thanks. I really appreciate that."

I hightail it out of there before Henry can get another urge.

A few days later we're ready for an outdoor Angel-greeting. We arrange for him to pull into our driveway while Henry waits near the mailbox. Henry goes rigid the moment the car arrives. Angel, wearing hat and sunglasses, climbs out, and Henry breaks into a barking hissy fit.

What's going on here? This is Angel. Surely Henry can smell his best pal?

With nothing to correct Henry but the pinch collar, I yank like a fisherman hauling in a sixty-five-pound striper and get him to settle down.

Angel waits, observing.

"Henn-ryyy!" He finally says in a happy voice. He sheds his glasses and hat, and waves the cap playfully. "Come here, Henry. How's my buddy?"

Henry's body breaks into curvy wiggles, and he about skips for joy. He jiggles his way to Angel and christens him with the ritual tinkle.

I'm over being embarrassed about that.

Mostly.

We go into the house, and I fill Angel in on Henry's misbehavior.

"Well, I told you about the shock collar not working as well. Henry also gets upset when the doorbell rings, or when people come into our house."

Angel nods. "Yeah, I could tell when I pulled up. Henry's stress was obvious."

Then he launches into a teaching session on how to read your dog's body language.

I take notes. Lots.

After that he gives Alan and me training exercises and announces we have to have practice doorbell rings.

My eyebrows pucker. "Practice rings?"

Chalk up another whacko thing we have to do for our whacko dog.

Angel takes Henry to the front door and makes him sit nearby. Then Angel slowly opens the door. "Now every time Henry makes a move—leaning, straining, whatever—toward the door, you close it. He'll learn that the door only opens when he's sitting nicely."

Henry leans. Angel shuts the door.

When Henry sits back again, Angel creaks the door open, at which point Henry thrusts out his nose. Angel closes the door in perfect rhythm. The cycle repeats three or four times before Henry catches on.

A smile spreads across my face. "Hey, I think we can do that!"

"Good. I want you to practice this several times a day. Send somebody outside with a treat, and when Henry is sitting under control, the person can come in and give him a treat. I want him to associate good things with people who ring the doorbell."

I look at Henry. "People bring yummy treats."

His ears perk at the *T* word. I perk too. Demented doorbell-drive has a cure.

"Let's take a look at the shock collar now. You say it's not working well?"

"It seems like Henry ignores it."

"Show me how you put it on him."

I wrangle Henry into the thing.

"That's how you always do it?" Angel pulls on the collar. "You've got it way too loose. The prongs have to have firm, constant contact with his skin."

"I guess we've just kept it where it always was. It used to work."

"These collars stretch out over time." He cinches in the collar a few holes.

"That tight?"

"You could probably go one notch more. Look." He sticks his finger under the collar. "See the play? You're not going to strangle him. It needs to sit high on his neck."

Where we never have it.

Angel picks up Henry's leash. "Let's have a look at the pinch collar now."

Yeah, we messed that up too. We'd added too many links as Henry's neck thickened into adult size. Angel removes the excess.

The shock collar fits right, the pinch collar fits right, and we're armed with doorbell exercises.

What can go wrong?

15

Jonathan has an unusual clothes habit. He wears shorts and T-shirts in the house no matter what the season. Every winter, I layer up in sweats and sit huddled by my little space heater while Jonathan runs around half naked. I suppose the key to understanding this is somewhere in the sit/run distinction, but that's not really the point here.

I wish he'd dress warmly, because looking at a kid in shorts when it's forty degrees outside can actually make you colder. Really. And there's only so close I can sit to my space heater before I catch fire. Still, I resist the urge to dress the kid because Alan says I have to let him make his own choices.

Whatever.

One afternoon, Jonathan and I are the only ones home, and it's time to get started on doorbell sessions with Henry.

"Jonathan, please come help with doorbell practice."

I'll spare you his comments about how thrilled he is to interrupt his movie to do dog training and his "Why can't Jacob do it?" griping. (Apparently the fact that Jacob isn't home doesn't constitute an acceptable excuse.)

"Get a treat. Then go through the garage and wait there a minute before you ring the bell."

"The garage? Why can't I go out the front door?"

"We have to make Henry think you're a stranger."

He rolls his eyes and turns to go.

"It's cold out there."

"I don't care."

Without bothering to put on socks, shoes, or a coat, he goes out the garage door. Twenty seconds later—*ding dong.*

So much for waiting a minute.

Henry makes a mad dash for the door.

I hit the zapper and scramble after him. "Phooey!"

No effect. Good grief, what's wrong with that thing?

"Sit, Henry! Sit!"

As if. What am I, the Dog Whisperer?

I capture Henry at the door, grab his collar, and make him sit . . . uh, try to make him sit. Eventually, he does.

The instant I crack the door, he's on his feet.

My palm smacks the door shut while the rest of my body works to get Henry back into a sit. This looks so easy when Angel does it.

While I struggle with the dog, I glimpse Jonathan through the little ripple-paned window on the door. He must be getting cold.

I finally force Henry's rump to the floor, and we start again. This time he leans the moment my hand touches the door handle.

I jerk my arm to my side.

Henry looks at me like I'm the lowest functioning pack member. His glare says, "Open the door, already. What part of this confuses you?"

My voice reaches for that firm, I'm-in-command tone. *"Blibe."* That's our bad German for "don't move, bucko."

Meanwhile, I see Jonathan start to pace on the door stoop.

I ease my hand toward the door, my glare glued to Henry's.

He itches to move, but I repeat my no-nonsense "Blibe." My fingers grope for the handle, gently thumb the latch, and pull.

Henry twitches but doesn't lean.

We have actual daylight now, pouring around the door. It's kind of gray, though. Apparently, while we've been messing around, it's started to drizzle outside.

I get the door open all of eight inches.

Henry tilts, just a touch. I close the door an inch. He looks up at me and tips back. I mirror his motion with the door. We seesaw our way along, working the opening inch by inch.

The door hits the halfway point, and Jonathan leans in.

"No!" I try not to screech, but it still comes out that way.

Henry leaps toward the door, and I kick it shut. I guess I should have checked whether Jonathan had gotten his nose out of the way first, but hey, the kid's got reflexes.

I pull Henry away from the door, drag him down the hall a few feet, and then try to circle him around so we can make a nice calm approach.

"It's cold out here," Jonathan hollers through the door.

Ya think?

I glance at the window. Jonathan hops from foot to foot on the frigid stoop.

Well, great. It's not like Henry can ignore a bouncing boy flickering across the pane. He jerks toward the enticing game.

"Stand still," I shout at Jonathan, with surprisingly little sympathy for his bare feet.

I wrestle with Henry until he puts his rear end down—one of those just-barely-sitting deals. We move through the whole seesaw process again. I get the door three-quarters open while Henry trembles on the ragged edge of obedience.

That's when Jonathan—apparently having had enough of his Siberian exile—tries to walk in.

I burst into action almost before the dog can. I shove Jonathan out the door, slam it in his face, and push Henry back to his spot. I feel like a three-handed ninja.

Jonathan's "Hey, wait!" protest still rings in my ears as I glower at the dog.

"Blibe!" My command is loud enough to be aimed at both of them.

But my steely determination ebbs. Good grief, I've hurled my possibly frostbitten child out the door in the rain, which is bad enough, but what if the neighbors have seen? Here's my shivering kid, pleading at the front door while I keep slamming it on him. Will I get a phone call from Child Protective Services? Worse, what if they ring the doorbell?

My whole body droops. "Henry, can we please get this right?"

He thrusts his nose forward and gives me a look that says, "Open the door, lady. Jonathan's out there, and I smell a treat."

He so doesn't care about my life.

I confess I don't strive for perfection on the next try. I need to get the poor kid in the house, and there's only so long Henry can survive "treat anticipation" before he turns into a complete mush-head.

I crack the door, and we teeter through another round. Henry gets away with far too much leaning—okay, lurching—especially when I finally let Jonathan come in with the treat. I grade us at about a *C* minus, and let's just say that's generous.

One practice down, and only, what? A thousand more to go? Oh, goody.

Henry's shock collar still perplexes me. Does the thing work or not? Sometimes it seems to affect him and sometimes not, even when I know we've correctly tightened it.

Once again I finger the little prongs. Someone has to test it. I think about paying the kids, but really, how would *that* look to Child Protective Services?

My gaze pins on Henry. "You're a pain, you know that?"

He wags his stubby tail and lays doe eyes on me that say, "Are you going to pet me now?"

I ruffle his velvet coat. Maybe he can't help it if he's instinctually rotten.

But a suspect shock collar still awaits me.

I drag in a deep breath and blow it out slowly. My fingers set the controller for the lowest possible setting. It'll only last a tenth of a second. Surely I can survive that.

I cringe, steel myself, and press the button.

Nothing happens. Good news. Well, sorta. I mean, my hand doesn't feel like it exploded or anything. But now I'll have to set the current higher.

Another deep breath, a cringe, a button pres—*ahh*!

Despite my scream, it's more of a startling buzz than a sting. It jars a memory of an awful test I'd once suffered. I'd mentioned to my doctor that my toes sometimes tingled and felt numb. The next thing I know I'm at a neurologist's office, hooked up to a machine that's zapping the muscles up and down my legs. Yeah, it hurt. Couldn't somebody have told me that was coming?

My nightmare flashback ends the shock collar test at level two. Hardly helpful. I can only suppose the thing works intermittently, and not at its original power. What next? Buy a new one?

Right. I won't zap myself, but I'm willing to inflict it upon my dog. What does that say about me? Getting a nutcase dog isn't bad enough, he has to show me uncomfortable truths about myself too. Then again, *I'm* not pitching hissy fits when a Fed Ex truck drives by.

The shock collar dilemma calls for much long, careful consideration, which is a fancy way of saying we avoid any sort of decision. Maybe something will miraculously change.

And one day, it does.

I'm upstairs using our weight bench. Don't get the wrong picture.

I'm not a body builder. But I do like to stay in shape, and for me, light weight work is a part of that.

Henry follows me upstairs because he thinks the weight bench is some big toy. I see his point. Moving parts, squeaky noise, what's not to love? He especially likes when I lie on my stomach. My legs pump iron while my face and hands are at the mercy of his sniffing nose. If I've washed recently, I get a slobbery tongue in the face. (Henry hasn't lost his soap fetish.)

Sometimes when I do butterfly lifts with free weights, I accidentally slam them together. These weights are really discs you're supposed to put on bars, but I'm too wimpy for that, so I just use the discs by themselves. Consequently, they clang together with a nice cymbal sound.

One day I make a particularly powerful clash, and Henry runs for cover.

Hmm. I think about all the construction in our neighborhood and how Henry shies away from the big, grinding trucks. Could it be that he doesn't like certain noises? Maybe I've discovered a new discipline tactic.

At K9 University, they once mentioned shaking coins in a can to startle a puppy out of bad behavior. That never worked on Henry. Well, he stopped—momentarily—then went right back to his evil destruction. We'd shake the can again, and he'd give us an irritated glance. The next shimmy got no response. Pretty soon we'd be writhing in convulsions with that stupid can because, hey, if we just rattled it harder it might work.

So much for that.

But with the weights, he definitely shows a serious aversion. It's worth a test.

I select a five-pound disc and a three-pound disc and put them near the front room windows. Henry sniffs the discs and gives me a one-eyed look that says, "Okaaaay. You're a little weird, but whatever."

Sometime later, an unsuspecting cat strolls through our yard, and Henry goes into tantrum mode, complete with clawing at the window. I snatch the weights, yell "Off," and smash the discs together as hard as I can.

A loud crash rings through the room. Even better, a high-frequency aftershock hangs in the air and tingles my ears. Henry's body sinks like someone cut five inches out of his legs. He slinks to me, his eyes flickering with a distressed, puckered look that says, "Please don't ever do that again."

Weapons of power! I almost cackle with glee.

My fingers clench the weights as if they might suddenly disappear. "Foose, Henry."

I walk out of the front room, and Henry follows like a well-trained dog. Imagine that.

I set the discs down in the living room and go to work on my writing. Henry, resigned to being good, lies on his blankie.

Half an hour later, some noisy truck rumbles down the road. Henry finds his feet and hits full stride in one step. Like a bull on fire, he charges down the hall toward the front room.

I chase after him. "Phooey!"

When he tries to make the sharp turn into the front room, his nails claw the wood floor.

Swell. New scratch marks. But at least the turn slows him down. By the time he gets into the room, he's lost half his momentum.

He skitters toward the window and jumps against it, barking his fool head off.

"Phooey!"

He doesn't even look at me.

What do I expect? I've left the weights in the living room.

I move in front of him to block the windows, so he starts barking at me. I advance toward him, and he launches into a backward pogo-dog thing. We clomp through the house until I get to the living room and scoop up the weights. I spread my arms wide, then—*CLANGGGGGGGGGG*!

Henry hits the ground in immediate submission.

Glory be, folks, we have a miracle.

My only mistake was not having the discs readily available. I truck upstairs and get another set. One for the living room, one for the front room. Hmm, maybe I ought to strew them all over the house? But then I won't have any for the actual weight bench. Funny, it doesn't strike me odd that I should scatter weights around for disciplining my dog. When did weird become normal for us?

Later that day, Henry decides it's playtime. He parks in front of the couch and lets loose with his never-ending, *barkbarkbark* demand.

"Phooey," I say automatically.

Right. Nothing happens except laughing—er, barking.

I pick up the weights.

His woof falters. Briefly. Then he gives me his stiff-bodied "You're gonna hafta make me" glare.

BarkBarkBarkBa—

CLANGGGGGGGGG!

His mouth clamps shut. He creeps to my feet and lies down with a glance that says, "Good gracious, lady, I didn't think you had it in you."

I look at the black discs of terror in my hands. Whoda thunk it? Free weights. And we paid how much for that shock collar?

A few days later, Jonathan's friend Cole rings the doorbell.

Naturally Henry throws a mush-headed fit.

A nice resounding clang forces him to calm down. We tell Cole to stay outside while Alan puts the pinch collar on Henry (we don't trust the shock collar). I hold the weights, Alan grips the leash, and we initiate doorbell practice number who-knows-what. Only this time, Cole waits on the other side of the door. Without a treat.

Jonathan eases the door open.

Henry leans, and Jonathan slams the door.

Guess we should've warned Cole about that.

Jonathan hurries to open the door again while I wave the weights in front of Henry's eyeballs. His head dips in dread, and his rump stays rooted to the floor.

The door gapes to reveal Cole's body fixed in a stiff should-I-run-from-these-people pose.

Alan winds the leash another time around his hand. "Come on in and greet Henry. I'm holding him."

Cole eyes the dog. Henry had been unwelcoming the last couple of times Cole appeared on our doorstep.

I sweep the weights in front of Henry's nose. "It's okay, Cole. Henry's afraid of the weights. He'll be fine with you."

Cole's gaze drifts to the discs, then to me.

He thinks I'm nuts. And yet, I can see him processing. The dog's not giving him an "I hate you" glare, we do seem to have control, but who ever heard of a fear of weights?

He gives a half shrug and walks over to Henry, who sniffs him nicely.

I keep the weights in full view.

Henry accepts—even enjoys—a pat from Cole, and then stands to rub his curvy body against the kid. The curvy body, we'd learned from Angel, is the key signal of Henry's acceptance.

Jonathan and Cole wander off, but I can't help finally feeling a little self-conscious. I guess it's kind of unorthodox to waggle the threat of weights at a dog. Maybe we should explore other loud noises for discipline.

The first thing that comes to mind is an air horn—those obnoxious noisemakers you hear at sporting events. Loud, screechy, piercing . . .

Perfect.

Because compared to clanging weight discs, blowing an air horn in some poor doorbell ringer's face isn't weird at all.

Over the next few weeks, Henry acts like a different dog. He actually listens when the weights are around. But after a couple of months, I sometimes have to clang them twice.

Then comes the day he launches into his *barkbarkbark* tirade, and I clash them once, twice, three times, then a fourth. He only sorta settles down, but my head jerks up at the acrid smell of smoke. Oh, goodness, maybe he's trying to warn us of a fire!

I drop the weights and whip my head around to the kitchen. No trouble there.

"Alan, I smell something burning!"

I storm to the next room, and then the next while Alan takes the opposite direction.

No smell, no smoke.

I turn, follow my nose back to the source, and end up meeting Alan at the weights.

We both sniff. Unmistakable odor taints the air.

Alan points at the weights. "What are these things made of?"

"Search me. But I get how people start fires with flint and steel now."

Is there a clause in my home insurance that covers me if I burn down our house with free weights?

Clearly, we've been relying on the discs a little too much. Their effect has dwindled, and they've become a potential fire hazard. Time to explore other options.

My next trip to Walmart finds me in the sporting goods aisle. Shouldn't an air horn be near the basketballs or something? I pace up and down the rows.

Finally a worker rambles toward me.

"Excuse me. I'm looking for an air horn. You know, one of those spray—"

"You mean this?" He points to a large can all of two feet from my nose.

"Um, yeah." My eyes skim over its generous length. If the thing had Lysol in it, you could disinfect an entire hospital. How am I going to carry it around in my pocket?

Will the noise even work on Henry? I hate to chuck a wad of cash at a possible epic failure.

I step back. "Do you have anything smaller?"

The man tips his chin in understanding, as if maybe I'm not a moron after all. "You mean for your boat?"

Why, why, WHY do people ask me these things?

"Uh . . . it's for my dog . . ."

He draws back with a wary, half tilt to his head.

I see that look a lot.

"Henry doesn't like loud noises . . . and it's kinda silly to use weights . . . being a fire hazard and all . . . I thought this might . . . work . . ."

He eyes me with bewildered concern.

Will more explanation help, or is it better to just leave it alone?

He picks up a little thing about the size of a pepper spray canister and wordlessly hands it over.

Hmm, nice and compact, but how many shrieks can I get out of it? I check the label. No help there. Maybe I won't need too many if Henry really hates it. I scan the shelf to find the price.

Five bucks? It's a teensy can filled with air.

I toss the world's most expensive mini horn in my cart and mumble some nonspecific word of thanks to the man.

When I get home, Henry is all nose.

"Yeah, you can sniff it, pal, but that won't prepare you for its dreaded powers. You're gonna hate this thing."

I hope.

The perfect test opportunity comes immediately. Henry had been trapped in his crate the whole time I'd shopped, and now his gaze transforms into a steely playtime-or-else stare.

BarkBarkBarkBarkBarkBarkBarkBarkBarkBarkBark.

I brandish my new weapon and press hard on the cap.

A breathy, vague *pphhhssssss* drizzles out.

Are you kidding me? Where's my piercing shriek?

Henry perks an ear for all of half a second.

I try again and get a teensy scream in the middle of much hissing. Henry's too busy barking to notice.

Maybe I need two hands. I hold the thing in one hand and smash the palm of my other hand on the cap. The top wobbles and comes down crooked. I try to push it straight but it tips off center the other way. The cap digs into my palm and rotates ineffectively.

What, they'd spent all their money on the air and couldn't afford to make a decent can?

Henry watches me grind that stupid piece of tin until it actually produces a semi-scream. The sound comes out as an alternating hiss and half-hearted whistle. Then it fizzles out.

Henry's head cocks sideways, and he stops barking to sniff my white-knuckled fingers.

Swell. I've distracted him with my throttling-the-can show. Assuming I can produce another moaning whistle, will it ever work as an actual deterrent? Doubtful, but no way am I going to waste five bucks.

The best thing to do is set him up, like Angel told us. I know just the temptation—one of his very most favorite things in the whole, wide world. Peanut butter.

Henry is a long-legged boxer, perfectly capable of reaching my kitchen countertops with his tongue. He plops his front legs on the granite and, voila, buffet time. For all our attempts at discipline, we've failed to eradicate this atrocity. Sometimes he snatches things and runs off with them, and sometimes he just licks stuff. If you ever come to my house, don't eat anything that's been left on the counter.

I pull the peanut butter from the pantry and smear a nice glob on a paper plate.

Henry's nose vacuums in the scent, and his drool boosts to a deluge.

With casual deliberateness, I leave the plate on the kitchen island and saunter into the living room.

Henry glues himself to my legs.

I hold out my hands. "I don't have it."

He passes his sniffer over my palms, wrinkles his forehead, and gives me a look that says, "Where, oh where, is my peanut butter?"

I sit on the couch, my back to the kitchen.

Henry totters a hesitant step away from me, then another. His nose aims him at the kitchen. His toenails click on the wood floor as he ambles toward the island, then stops.

Sniff . . . sniff . . . sniff.

Oh, yeah. He knows it's there.

Click . . . click . . . click. He circles the island and stops again.

I can't help a little peek into the kitchen. I ease myself around and lift my head to see over the breakfast bar.

Henry stands next to the island. Doing nothing. Then he swings his head toward me.

I duck.

Oh my gosh, I'm spying on my dog. Have I sunk that low?

Apparently.

I crouch, motionless.

All is quiet. Then click . . . click . . . click around the island again.

Anytime now I'll hear a rustle of movement and his paws hitting the countertop.

Nothing happens.

I peek again.

Henry stares back at me with a sad "Why aren't you giving me the peanut butter?" gaze.

That's just plain dirty fighting.

I whirl away from him, fold my arms across my chest, and plunk on the couch.

Click . . . click . . . click . . .

Henry heads for the kitchen table. He grazes to and fro, snorting along the floor and slurping crumbs until I lose track of exactly where he is.

Rats. I'll have to peek again. I repeat my stealth turn-and-lift, but I can't see the dog.

Great, because I don't have anything else to do all day but play hide-and-seek with my hound. Oh, for some exploding peanut butter that would screech like a mutant siren when Henry's paws hit the counter. Why does nobody invent these practical things?

I creep off the couch, duck alongside the breakfast bar, and cautiously peer over it.

Henry meanders at the other end of the kitchen, still looking for stray food. How can he ignore the call of the peanut butter?

As if he hears my thought, his head jerks up.

I drop to the floor.

Ouch.

Mental note: I make a lousy spy. Do not go pro.

Henry trots out of the kitchen.

So much for that. He's clearly suspicious.

I go back to the couch, pick up my laptop, and pretend to work. Henry wanders into the front room, but he saunters back to the kitchen before long.

Aha. Now I'll get him. Surely he doesn't remember my secret plot. He'll find the peanut butter and gobble it. Then I'll smash the button on my magic shriek-maker (which will hopefully shriek) and cure him of thievery.

Click . . . click . . . click . . . around the island. Sniff . . . sniff . . . sniff.

I grasp the little can and ready myself for a two-handed attack.

Henry plods out of the kitchen.

Not possible.

Just not.

That dog has swiped muffins, steak, napkins, Tupperware, butter, bread, dough, pizza, cookies, salami, and countless other things off that counter. I only have to turn my back. But when I plant his favorite thing to trap him, I finally get Lassie?

There's got to be some God-given instinct telling him when I'm setting him up and when I'm truly clueless. I refuse to admit he can be that smart.

After fifteen more minutes, my last tendril of hope abandons me. I sulk into the kitchen and eye the peanut butter. What am I supposed to do with it now?

Henry trots in.

I admit it. I want to throw the stuff away right in front of his nose. But how can I punish him for being good?

I stalk through the house, snatch his Kong toy, smear the peanut butter inside, and stiffly hand it over. He hits me with his "Oh-happy-day" face and scoots off with the Kong.

How is it this dog can finally do something admirable and still manage to exasperate me?

16

It's not always a good thing when everyone in the neighborhood knows your dog. One evening, while Henry and I are out walking, a truck pulls alongside us and stops.

The driver rolls down his window. "I see you finally caught your dog."

I stare blankly at the man. Henry isn't the kind of dog you can let out of your sight, so he's either on a leash, in our fenced yard, or in our house.

The driver frowns. "That's the dog that keeps getting away, isn't it?" He says this like the answer is obvious. "It's always getting into my garbage, but I can never catch it."

Finally I put it all together. The guy is mistaking Henry for a wandering stray. I've had a glimpse or two of that dog roving in the newest, mostly dirt phase of the neighborhood. The poor hound looked ragged and weatherworn, and never got within thirty yards of us. Certainly never close enough that we could do anything about it. I have the vague notion it has boxer in its blood, and it's brown like Henry.

"You must be talking about that stray. That's not our dog."

"Uhh huuhh." The man pastes on an I-don't-believe-you-but-I'll-be-polite smile.

My shoulders stiffen. "Our dog has white on his face and neck.

The stray doesn't. I've seen it a few times, but I don't know where it came from."

"Mmm hmm." His expression doesn't change, and he drives off.

I look at Henry. He looks at me. I suppose I can't blame Henry for this. But how much trouble has that stray been causing? Worse, does the whole neighborhood think it's our dog? I better pay attention if I see that stray again.

My opportunity comes the next morning. I get a late start on a bike ride around the subdivision, so rather than enjoying the cool air of sunrise, I prickle with August sweat. My mood doesn't need the stray, but there the dog stands, eyeing me across the sun-dried landscape like a scene from a grade-B Western.

I brake and peer back.

Definitely a boxer—a female. Furthermore, she wears a faded collar without tags. Hmm. Maybe not a homeless stray, but somebody's lost dog.

Despite the whole grumpy, prickly sweat thing, I do my best to muster a happy voice. "Here, girl."

Stone-faced, she stares at me.

Obviously, she needs a more appealing enticement: food.

Which I don't have.

I'm on the fringe of the neighborhood. Do I go all the way home for a lure, or let her keep ransacking people's garbage cans?

Why does the right answer always have to be the inconvenient one?

I pedal home, stuff my pockets with cheese and turkey, grab a spare leash and a big bone, and dash back outside. August swelter hits me anew, like maybe someone cranked up the heat when I wasn't looking.

My hands sweat on my bike grips. I pedal back across the neighborhood to where I left the stray.

She's gone.

My hackles go up. She's disrupted my exercise when I'm already running late, caused me to race home for food, and now she's going to leave me with a pocketful of melting cheese? I don't think so.

I scour the area. Ten minutes later, I discover her in a big, grassy median. I ditch my bike and sidle closer.

She drifts away.

I break out the food and let her catch a whiff.

Ah, that gets her attention. She pads closer, then stops, too afraid to continue, too hungry to run off.

I see ticks hanging on her, and my heart wrenches.

She needs me.

I pull out my shredded cheddar and pitch the whole lot. She pounces, devours it.

Next I open the turkey, aim for halfway between us, then toss. She edges nearer. One step, then two.

I cast another bit—a double prize if she'll come a few feet farther. She does.

I flick yet another piece. She slinks low, her gaze darting from the turkey to me. With a quick lunge, she snatches the morsel. I drop half a slice right near my feet.

Then a truck roars up behind us.

The driver juts his chin out the open window. "That your dog?" He eyes her like she has the mange, which she actually might. "Can't you keep it locked up? It digs up my yard and gets in the garbage. Bugs the neighbors too. We keep trying to catch it but it's too quick."

"She's a stray."

"Haven't I seen you walking that dog?" He doesn't veil the suspicion in his tone.

I sigh. "Ours is a male with white on his face."

A frown still puckers the man's features as he drives off.

I need to catch this dog before the homeowners association lynches us. When I turn, I see my troublemaker has skittered thirty feet away.

I sling another piece of turkey, and we start the dance again. This time, when I get her within my reach, I make a grab.

Her eyes glaze with pure survival instinct, and she vaults away.

But I live with Henry, the world's most elusive dog, and I've amassed a heap of dog-catching tactics. I filter through my options and decide on the gentle approach with a humdinger lure. I pull out a big honkin' bone.

She gets a whiff and clearly decides to take desperate action. She flashes her sharp, pointy teeth, then barks, growls, and even lunges at me.

Anyone driving by would think I'm insane to stand here holding a bone in front of a raging dog, but I live with Henry, supreme dictator wannabe. I recognize the bully game immediately. She acts so much like Henry that I can't manufacture one ounce of fright. Be it God-given bravery or bone-headed stupidity, I stand firm and call her bluff.

After nearly forever, she backs away, tongue lolling, sides heaving. She looks longingly at the bone, then settles under a scrappy tree with barely enough shade for her and none for me.

I dangle the bait and edge closer.

She lifts her head. Her gaze flits back and forth, and her muscles twitch with the need to bolt.

I sit on the spiky grass and wait. A very, very, very long time.

Then I feel a stinging bite on my ankle, followed by two more. An ant colony.

The minutes crawl, much like the ants. Little Miss Immune to Insects watches as I scratch at my prickly sweat, smack bugs, and inch closer to her.

Every time she frets, I slow the pace.

More minutes. More ant bites. More edging.

The sun bakes.

I try singing to her.

She gives me a one-browed "You gotta be kidding me" look. I'm a lousy singer. And I feel really stupid.

Silence stretches between us, even as my body closes the distance. I ease my hand to her dirty fur. Her eyes widen, but she stays put. I give her several calming strokes, then grab the collar.

She yelps, leaps, whirls, and snaps at my hand. But I live with Henry, king of the collar nippers, so I don't flinch. I've learned how to hold fast to the collar while protecting my limbs.

She struggles a while more before she rolls in submission.

I snap on a leash and look her over. Other than a preponderance of hanging ticks and a desperate need for a bath, she appears sound. I scan her worn collar for tags.

Nothing.

The last possibility is a microchip.

I tow her home, load her in the car, and drive to the local PetCo. Hopefully they have a chip reader.

Miss Lost Her Way behaves well through the whole deal. Nothing like the rampaging beast she'd feigned.

The friendly workers at PetCo are happy to check for a chip. The scan comes up blank.

"Do you mind trying again? Our dog's microchip has slipped from where it ought to be. Maybe hers has too?"

"I don't know if that would matter, but I'll try again." The guy waves the reader over the top of her neck and down both shoulders. "Sorry. Nothing."

"All that work to catch her, and now I can't even get her home."

"Let me try one more time. Sometimes it doesn't read right."

This time he waves the wand all over. "Yep, there it is."

I literally slump with relief. As I walk out the door, I dial the owner, whose response is not at all what I anticipated. She sounds not quite sober, her speech a bit slurred, and she seems slow to grasp that I've found her dog.

I pull out of the parking lot, still trying to explain the situation to the gal. I'm SO not giving her my address. Who drinks at 11:00 a.m.?

I ask her to describe her car, and we agree to meet at a gas station in twenty minutes. But I still have reservations. I mean, does this person have any business owning a dog? To be safe, I go home and get Alan first. He has a remarkable radar for unstable people.

We pull into the station and wait.

Pretty soon the dog owner's car rolls up. When the young woman steps out, all our reservation fades. It isn't alcohol that interferes with her communication. Tears pour nonstop down her face.

"I can't believe it." She gathers the dog in her arms. "It's been eight months . . . she jumped my fence . . . I had to move . . . how did you . . ."

Over their joyful reunion, I share how I'd captured the dog.

"I never thought I'd see her again. I don't know how I can thank you."

As if this scene isn't thanks enough? I wipe my own tear-filled eyes. "No problem. I'm just glad we got her back to you."

Good grief, was it all because of Henry? Whoda thunk it?

Black skies. Shrieking wind. Trees whipping in three directions at once.

It's one of *those* days in Oklahoma. The kind where everyone tunes to the weather broadcast to find out where the next twister will hit. Some never drop from the clouds. Some swoop down and turn whole neighborhoods into a giant game of Pick-up Sticks.

I will never get used to it.

Then there are the sirens. I understand they need to be loud, and they can't play "Happy Birthday," but must they so accurately mimic air-raid sirens? I feel like I'm in the blitzkrieg every time they screech—even when the tornado heads for the boonies on the other side of the county.

Today it's coming straight at me.

Henry and I are home alone. The boys are in school, and Alan's at work, all out of harm's way. I'm thankful for that. And I'm thankful for my storm shelter, even if it *does* feel like a steel sarcophagus.

For the last ten minutes I've been gathering my things—wallet, keys, phone, laptop—to take with me into the shelter. Henry glues himself to my heels because this looks like the C-A-R routine.

I check the TV one more time. The tornado hasn't dropped from the sky, but the weatherman still urges everyone in its path to take shelter.

"That's us, Henry."

His ears perk, and he stares at me like he can make the words "Let's go for a ride" come out of my mouth. Instead I grab his leash and a flashlight.

He leaps and runs for the door. A walk is even better than the car.

I wrangle the leash onto his dancing body. We're not going far—only into the garage—but I need him close. We have maybe eight minutes before the tornado is overhead, and I don't want to scramble to catch him when the time comes.

In the garage, Henry pulls toward the door we go out when we walk.

"Sure, Henry. Let's take a trot around the lake. We can get pelted by hail and maybe sucked up in a wind vortex."

He gives me an eager, "I'm all for it" look.

I wish I could be all for it too. The garage is dark, and the shelter—a long, skinny thing under the floor—is darker yet. I move to it and slide the steel door open.

Eeew! Bad, bad smell. Like something died in there. I think this in the cliché sense, but then my eyes go wide. Something really *could* have died in there.

Hmm.

Maybe the tornado won't come.

Right.

I shine my flashlight inside the shelter. There's a strange little blob on the floor. I don't really want to know, but then, I don't want to go into a cramped little cave with a stinky, unidentified blob, either.

I squint. That'll make it seem less horrible.

Not.

It's a dead mouse just sort of sprawling there. Not shriveled or anything—it almost could have been sleeping except for that certain dead look dead things have.

I go down a couple of steps, but I can't force myself to go to the bottom of the shelter. If I stay on the stairs I won't be sharing a tomb-like structure with a dead thing.

Unfortunately, the portable TV is at the far end of the shelter. And I need it. How else can I know when it's safe to come out? Or when I absolutely can't wait another minute and must go in and shut the door?

I look at Henry. He looks at me. His eyes say, "I don't know what you're doing, but ain't no way I'm comin'."

So much for getting Lassie to fetch the TV.

I hold my breath and turn my back to the little blob. Then I climb down, slink over, and grab the TV. I get the willies all over again as I scramble out.

For the next couple of minutes I sit on a wobbly two-by-six stair, watching the screen and holding Henry's leash.

He stands as far from the hole as possible. For once, we're in complete agreement. Nothing short of an F5 roaring up the driveway will get us into that shelter.

The radar on TV shifts to a red and green wind-shear view. Pretty colors that mean bad things. Three more glowing rings—tornado rotations—pop up on the radar. They're strewn about the county, and the sirens shriek anew.

Henry's gaze circles the garage, then pins back to me. He doesn't get antsy, doesn't pull away, doesn't bark to play. He just stands there. With me. Like an actual companion.

It's odd not being at odds with the dog. Odder still to comfort each other. I savor it for another minute or two, but there's still a tornado heading our way.

I don't have a clue how to bring Henry safely into the shelter. I can't just toss him into the hole—it's a five-foot drop. The stairs are too narrow for him to use and too unstable for me to carry him down.

But I *will* get him in.

And it's time.

I pull Henry closer and take one last look at the screen. It's a sea of angry color. At the bottom of the storm's mass—in the hook, they call it—looms the glowing circle.

Then it simply vanishes before my eyes.

Tornado done.

I stare at the TV, but I know very well how twisters work. They form, they live, they die in seconds, minutes, or hours.

This one died.

For another moment, I can't even move. Then I backpedal out of the hole and slam the shelter door shut.

Yes, I'm leaving the mouse for Alan to deal with. I clean toilets, he picks up dead things. It's kind of a rule.

Henry watches me drop in a bolt to lock the door. He gives the whole assembly—lock, bolt, handle—the once-over with his sniffer, then steps back.

Again our gazes meet.

Ordeal survived. Together.

If we could just have a weather crisis every day, we'd have a great relationship.

17

I love the windows of our house that face the backyard and the stand of trees beyond. Something about an eyeful of wilderness soothes me. Then again, I don't expect to glance out one day and see Henry barreling toward the window.

I don't have time to finish thinking, "Oh, bad," before the glass explodes.

There's no point asking what in the world Henry was thinking. It's not like he'll develop speech and tell me. One minute he's milling about the backyard, the next—kablooey.

He heard a bunny in the front yard, kicked into pursuit, and figured he'd crash through the house to save time? He forgot where the back door is? He wondered what it'd be like to blow our window to smithereens?

It's not that he's never jumped against the window; it's that he's never jacked into warp speed and hurled himself at it.

Until now.

The next picture I have is Henry on the rebound eight feet back from the gaping window place, wearing a vacant look. I don't know how he can smash the window clean through and still bounce backward off it.

The good news? He isn't a bloody pulp on the ground.

On the downside, jagged glass rings the spot where my window used to be, and the rest of the glass lies spewed in a gazillion pieces across my patio and living room furniture. Exactly how is it possible for projectile glass to spray both inside and outside at once? My face parks itself in a shell-shocked look that rivals Henry's.

I open the door. Henry stands on all fours, now fifteen feet from the patio. No blood. No dangling body parts. Just the mindless look.

That won't last long. Henry's mutant curiosity gene will surely propel him into the glassy sea.

I set off in search of my shoes, and by the time I find them, Henry has moved out of sight around the corner of the house. Just as well. I don't want him crunching through shards.

I take a deep breath and survey the disaster. Amazing, really, the incredible variety of glass shard sizes and shapes you notice when you're wondering how you're going to clean them up.

I close my eyes, but the mess doesn't go away. Worse, I have twenty minutes before I need to take Jonathan and his friend to a slumber party. And I have a hole in my house.

As I process that disconcerting bit of data, an instinct prickles me—the mother thing that kicks in when the kids are way too quiet and you know they're plotting evil. I figure I better check on Henry before I tackle the Nightmare on Patio Street.

I venture around the side of the house and spot Henry in a stiff, head-down posture that screams trauma. My lungs quit exchanging air.

Henry turns his head and stares at me, his eyes glassy.

I lurch closer and glimpse the backside of his front leg—a mass of red, oozing blood.

I will my lungs to work again. Oozing is good. Well, relatively. Spurting scarlet fountains would be far worse.

Henry totters to the right.

My mind fixates on two things: Get him down. Stop the bleeding.

I chug to his side, kneel, and discover a hideous laceration—sickeningly long—down the back of his leg. With careful hands, I try to tip him over.

He resists.

Instinct? Stubbornness? Insane plot to spew blood in every corner of the yard?

The threat of shock grows.

Jonathan arrives on the scene.

"Go inside and get me a damp towel." I try not to let my voice shake.

"Is . . . is he okay?"

"I think so, but we need to stop the bleeding. Run."

Okay, so maybe a damp towel isn't the most logical choice. But I had a glimpse of Henry's wide-open wound. I imagine thousands of towel fibers stuck to dog innards—parts meant to stay buried under skin and fur, not glued to some terry cloth bandage. I figure the dampness will keep it from sticking. (Or I have a Great-Grandma moment. She's from the old country. Learned to speak English in kindergarten. Once prescribed a barbecued pork bone—complete with sauce—for my cranky three-month-old son. I attribute most of my irrational thoughts to genetics.)

"Hurry!" I call to Jonathan. It's not like he won't hear me. The window is gone.

He comes running back with one of my nice kitchen towels. A dainty, white one.

Any person with two X chromosomes would never have chosen such a thing. She would have instinctively grasped the limitations of a washing machine, and had she been so incapacitated that she could forage no farther than the kitchen, those X chromosomes would have driven her to the oldest, ugliest towel in the drawer.

I try to be patient. "Couldn't you have gotten one of Henry's bath towels?"

"You said hurry."

Okay, shouldn't have done that. At least it's wet.

Henry is standing, so I straddle him to keep him from bolting. This isn't going to be pleasant.

"Mom, I can't look at this." Jonathan's voice is low with distress. "Would you go find my phone? I have to call the vet."

He scurries off. I can't blame him for not wanting to see Henry like this. I don't want to see it either.

I bend down, wrap the towel around his leg, and try to hold it in place. How am I going to get him to the vet when I have to pick up my son's friend and take them to a sleepover? And if that isn't enough, Alan drove the junky van to deliver Jacob to a baseball game.

I have the pristine, barely driven, not-a-scratch-on-it car.

Good-bye shiny, leather seats.

Henry shuffles, clearly in pain.

I don't dare remove the towel, but how can I get him to lie down while holding it in place?

Jonathan arrives, breathless, with both the phone and the phone book. "I thought you'd need the vet's number."

"Smart thinking, Jonathan, thanks. But I've got it in my cell." Of course I have the number in my cell. It's a wonder it isn't on speed dial.

I flip the phone open but don't dial the vet. Alan first. Poor, unsuspecting man.

He picks up, and I cut off his greeting. "Hon, you've gotta get home. Henry smashed the window. Glass everywhere. Tore up his leg. Blood. Don't know where else he's hurt. Gotta get him to the vet."

Bless my husband's former EMT training. His calm voice comes right back at me. "Have you called the vet yet?"

"Next call. Had to give you the heads-up."

"Okay. Call them now, then call me back."

Easy for him to say. He's not hunched over a restless, bleeding dog, trying to hold an attractive, formerly white towel around a lacerated leg.

After my clumsy dialing job, a happy voice greets me. "Meadows Veterinary Clinic."

Breathless, I clip out the disastrous facts.

"Oh, that's terrible," the gal says (and I hadn't even told her about my shiny leather seats), "but we're closed right now."

I squeeze my eyes shut. Leave it to Henry to maim himself at 5:00 p.m. on a Friday.

"You'll need to take him to an after-hours veterinary hospital. We usually recommend the one on Stanford Avenue. Subeel Vet—"

The phone slips. I fumble, then jerk it back to my ear.

The voice continues. "—need the phone number?"

"Number? Yes, please."

She rattles off a number.

Henry, eerily silent, shifts his weight. I ought to get him off his leg. Maybe—

The woman's voice pokes into my thoughts. "Got that?"

"Uh . . . what was that number again?"

She repeats it, but the moment she finishes, all traces vacate my brain.

"I'm sorry. I need that one more time." My IQ is shrinking by the second.

"Okaaay." She repeats the number.

"That's . . . um . . ."

This is ridiculous. I can remember a number. I can remember what the grocery store charged for reduced fat Cheez-Its last week. I know when their "new low price" is a rip-off because it isn't lower than last year's price increase. I remember my telephone number from two houses back. I get numbers.

I just can't remember this emergency number. That's why 911 is so cleverly *simple*.

My desperate gaze falls on my son. "Jonathan! Help me remember this number."

By now the woman on the phone has to wonder how I survived to adulthood, and worse, had the gall to procreate. With the patience of the next Mother Teresa, she starts again.

I mouth the first three numbers to Jonathan, which he dutifully repeats just as she says the last four.

Yes, I ask her for them yet again.

Her voice gets that make-the-panicky-lady-understand tone. "4 . . . 8 . . . 3 . . . 2."

"4832. Got it. 4832. Thank you. 4832. Bye." I don't know which of us is more relieved.

She probably sat at her desk five full minutes waiting for me to call back and ask for the number again. Of course, I have the phone book. I can look it up. Except the name of the place she recommended went out of my mind long before the number. Maybe I can blame this on the blood rushing to my head as I stoop over my dog.

"Okay, Jonathan, give me your part."

He comes through with no trouble, and he'd gotten his numbers only once. I'd feel crummy about myself if I had time. Instead, I get my part in, and soon the pet ER is ringing. We have a brief exchange, the gist being: Get the dog here now.

I mention the wet towel before I hang up.

"Wet?" Her tone lands just shy of horrified. "That hinders blood clotting. Gauze would be much better."

"Gauze? Okay, thanks."

Great. We don't have dog-gauze. Where would you get that anyway? Not that it matters. It isn't like I can dash off to the store right now.

I smack my phone shut and look up. Where did Jonathan go?

In answer to my unspoken question, he comes jogging around the corner of the house, our first-aid kit in his hand.

Oh, clever boy. People-gauze! It just might work. But is it okay to use people-gauze on a dog? Surely in an emergency?

Duh.

I may not be the first person you want to call in a crisis.

I'll say one thing about the damp towel. It doesn't stick. I toss it aside and try to pretend my shiny, leather seats won't go the way of the pretty, white towel.

Then Henry begins to tremble. I can live my whole life without seeing the inner parts of his wide-open leg again. My leather seats lose all importance. I wrap his wound with people-gauze—the whole roll—then try yet again to make him lie down.

Naturally, he resists.

We have a gentle tussle, if such a thing exists, but I finally cradle him to the ground. Unfortunately, I pin my legs underneath him. Perhaps I should have planned that better, but I have more important things to consider, like getting Henry to the vet and dealing with my son and his friend's sleepover.

Maybe the boy's parents can drive instead. They'll understand changing the plan on short notice. They know Henry.

I flip my phone open and dial.

The boy's dad barely gets a hello out before I spew. "I'm sorry about this, but can you possibly take the boys to the sleepover? I've got to get Henry to the vet. He smashed our window."

"Oh, no! Is he okay?"

I give Henry a soothing stroke. "I hope so, but his leg is torn up. I'm sitting out in the yard with him."

"He went all the way through?"

"Not exactly. He shattered it and bounced back."

"He was outside . . . trying to get in?"

"Yup."

The line goes quiet for a moment or two. "Why?"

"No telling."

"Well, don't worry about the boys. I'll get them. You just take care of Henry."

I thank him, then dial Alan.

"What's happening?" he says without a hello.

"I called the vet. They're closed. We need to take Henry to an emergency clinic."

"Which one?"

"Um . . ." Oh dear. Not this again. I scrunch my eyeballs into my head. Maybe I can squeeze the name out the backside of my brain.

"Shumie . . . Subie . . . something like that. It's on Stanford. I know that."

"Okay. I've left Jacob at his baseball game. I'm on my way home. I need to be back in an hour to get him, but I can take Jonathan and his buddy to the sleepover."

"No, I called his dad. He'll drive."

"How's Henry?"

"Shaking in my lap. I don't know where else he's hurt, and I can't fathom him walking on his leg. We need to carry him to the car."

We both know the royal "we" means "you." It's not like I can dead-lift sixty-five pounds of injured dog off my lap without damaging one or both of us.

"I'm ten minutes away."

"Hurry."

Every second drags. Henry droops, eerily silent.

All I can do is wait. And worry. And wonder if the hideous laceration is only the beginning of the injuries we'll discover. I mean, smashing full speed into a window can't be good for the proper care and maintenance of dog innards.

I stroke Henry's soft fur. "It's going to be okay." I hope.

Where in the world is Alan?

And what is that smell?

Oh dear. I recognize it. So the real question is, does that distinctive doggie-doo odor emanate from directly beneath me or just somewhere very close?

And is that dampness on my backside related to the smell?

Given that my legs are pinned, I turn my head as far as I can in both directions. Surely I'll see a pile nearby.

Or not.

New question. Will I have time to change clothes before going to the vet or should I, for the sake of the emergency, travel with doggie-doo hanging off my derriere?

I shut my eyes and hope I'm merely sitting in a benign patch of moist ground.

An eon later, Alan rounds the corner of the house. Henry doesn't stir.

"Hi, guy." Alan bends over him. "What'd you do?"

No tail wag. No face lick.

Alan stands. "I'll take him out the gate. I don't want to go through the house. There's glass everywhere."

"Glass everywhere" doesn't actually do justice to the glass-shard blizzard that hurtled across the patio and carved disaster through the living room.

"We better drive him in the van." Alan heads for the house. "Henry can lie down in back. I'll throw in a blanket."

Uh-oh. Only one X chromosome. "Get his junky brown blanket," I call. Maybe he wouldn't have snatched our bedspread, but why risk it? The good news is that we can use the van—by far the preferred mode of travel when blood is involved.

Alan returns and, with a grunt, hefts Henry into his arms.

"Open the gate." He staggers a bit under the dog's weight.

My legs are asleep and refuse to cooperate.

"Hurry."

Simple, if my legs could function. I take a deep breath and find a way to stand. After three stumbling steps, that horrid pins and needles thing hits full force.

"Come on." Alan's well ahead of me, approaching the gate.

I'm sympathetic to his hauling sixty-five pounds in his arms, but has he ever tried to run on needle legs? I don't think so. Still, I scrinch up my face, invent a new Olympic event (the twenty-yard awkward dash), and bust the gate open.

As we settle Henry in the van, we formulate our plan. I'll take Henry while Alan cleans the glass, does what he can to cover the window, and then picks up Jacob in the car.

I no sooner get out of the driveway than Henry pops up and limps a lap around the van's interior.

"Oh my gosh, Henry! Get off your leg!"

Why do I think he'll understand that?

I certainly understand his answer though: slobber, slobber, sniff the window, check the other window, check the back window, slobber, slobber, sniff.

"All right, Henry. Are you on death's door or not? Make up your mind."

He goes for the Ping-Pong routine. Albeit in slow motion. Still, I know what that gash looks like.

"Get off your leg, Henry."

Slobber, slobber, window, window.

At least my worries about how I'm going to get him into the vet's office dissipate. He has a horrid limp, but he can walk.

I take a whiff of the air and discover more good news. The distinctive doggie-doo odor hasn't followed us. Things are looking up.

When we arrive, Henry hops right out, eager to explore. First, he waters the bushes outside. You have to wonder how those poor shrubs survive the incessant parade of piddling dogs. Then he barges through the clinic doors, which I barely get open in time.

Finally, as I stand at the desk to explain what happened, Henry yanks away at the leash, trying to track every scent and befriend every creature in the entire building.

And I'm worried he sustained internal injuries?

The veterinary technician squints at me. "He jumped through a window?"

"Not all the way. He smashed it, then bounced back."

"Wow. He must have seen something outside."

"Well, no . . . he was already outside."

"He tried to jump *into* the house?"

I give a half nod without meeting her gaze.

"Why?"

As if I know? Really, people, he didn't say.

Despite Henry's curious façade, I can see trauma lurking underneath. By the time we get to the exam room, his blood seeps through the gauze, and his behavior is subdued.

"He jumped through a window?" It's the vet who's squinting at me now.

I cut to the chase. "I don't know why."

"Poor guy." She eases her hand toward Henry.

He jerks his head upright.

She freezes. "He'll bite?"

He's never once snapped at a vet. He's usually Pollyanna in short brown fur, even when they're poking a thermometer up his rear. But he's clearly stressed and in pain, so I can't rule out the possibility. "Not viciously. But maybe to keep you away from his wound."

"We'll need to muzzle him."

My shoulders droop, but I nod. "He'll take it best from me."

There's something horrible about stripping away another creature's defense, leaving it completely vulnerable, forcing trust at the highest level. Do I have the right?

I eye his leg. No choice.

Wordlessly, she hands me the muzzle. I turn it over in my hands, my fingers running along the mesh. Strong, but breathable. I give Henry's snout a gentle caress, willing him to trust me. "I'm sorry." My words come out whispered. I slip on the muzzle and brave the sorrow and confusion in his eyes.

The vet peels the gauze—all seven feet of it—and lets out a long breath.

Not good. Henry has two lacerations with a tiny strip of fragile skin between. She isn't sure it will hold up to sutures. She wants to take him to their treatment area, wash the wound, and reevaluate.

I swallow a huge lump in my throat. "I'd like to go with him. Henry might be more comfortable with me there."

She eyes me.

For the first time, I notice Henry's bloodstains on my clothes. I don't know if it's that, or just something in my face that makes her go against standard policy and agree. Then she rifles through a drawer of supplies and nabs a fresh roll of dog-gauze.

My eyebrows hike in admiration. They have a pile of the stuff. Of course they would. They're a pet hospital. I open my mouth to ask where they got it, when a peculiar observation strikes. That dog-gauze package looks awfully similar to the people-gauze I used at home.

There's a proverb in the Bible that says even a fool is thought wise if he keeps silent. I clamp my mouth shut quicker than a bicyclist in a cloud of gnats.

She swiftly rewraps his leg, then leads us to a large back room filled with tables, crates, and wounded animals. Once again, Henry begins to tremble. She injects him with a painkiller, then gives it some time to work. Even so, he cries when she and another tech lift his bulk to the washing table.

I press my lips together, holding in a useless plea for an exam that won't hurt him.

He cries when she runs water over his wound.

Tears burn my eyes.

He cries when she probes his wound, scrutinizing for treatment options.

I squeeze my hands into powerless fists.

He cries, and my heart shatters to smithereens.

Anesthesia. Sutures. That's the plan.

As the tech turns me toward the little room where they tell you the financial repercussions of your pet disaster and make you sign your life away, a new tech saunters into the room. "Dr. Benson, do you think you could look at a duck?"

The vet frowns. "A duck?"

"Yeah. It's got an abscess on its head."

I wonder how this can be an emergency on a Friday night, and I guess the vet does too.

"Is it . . . dying?" she says, not unkindly.

"I don't know. The duck's owners wanted to see Dr. Kell, but she said you had more experience with, um, waterfowl. Will you see it?"

The vet shrugs. "Sure."

Strange what goes on behind the scenes at a vet clinic. I can only hope Henry and the duck don't have an unfortunate meeting. After Henry's leap of lunacy from the pontoon boat, how do I know he doesn't have a vendetta against the entire species?

The vet gets another shot ready for Henry. This one is a happy-loopy drug. I watch his eyes go from worried predator to blissful resident of La-La Land. My whole body unclenches itself.

The vet turns to me. "I'm afraid you can't stay while we suture his leg. After you sign the papers, you may as well go home. We have some other emergencies to tend to before Henry's."

What, the duck with the abscess? Surely not?

I scan the room again. Lethargic creatures lie in crates, tubes and equipment protruding here and there. Okay, maybe there are a few animals worse off than Henry.

"We'll call you when we're finished." The vet glances down at her jacket. She, too, sports Henry's blood. "Hmm. I guess I'd better change. No one wants a blood-covered vet coming at her pet. It doesn't inspire confidence."

A vet with a sense of humor. The perfect person to work on Henry.

After a last look at my seriously doped-up doggie, I follow the tech out. She hands me an eye-popping estimate.

Even with sticker shock hampering my mental competence, I notice the drive home, sans Hurricane Henry, feels far too quiet.

18

The hours trickle away. What's taking so long? Henry's surgery should be long over.

I dial the hospital. "How's Henry doing?"

"Sorry. This is taking longer than we expected. We've had two other emergencies, but Henry's next. We'll be starting anytime now."

I refrain from asking about the duck and hang up to wait some more.

Somewhere around 11:00 p.m., the call comes.

"Henry's just waking from the anesthesia. Dr. Benson sutured his leg and feels it has a good chance of holding together. Did you want Henry to stay the night or were you going to pick him up? He'll be fine to travel. You could come now."

Hmm, do I detect a please-get-this-dog-off-our-hands sentiment? "Of course we'll come get him if that's what you think is best."

"I'm sure he'll be more comfortable at home." The tech sounds relieved. "He wasn't happy by the time we put him under . . ."

Ah. Henry's happy-loopy obviously wore off before they got him anesthetized. I could only imagine the ruckus he'd created.

I think we make the twenty-five-minute trip in seventeen flat. They usher Alan, Jacob, and me into the treatment area, where we find Henry crashed out with a giant plastic cone around his neck to prevent wound-licking. Hadn't they said he was awake?

I stroke his fur. "Henry?"

An incognizant eye flickers open.

The tech nods at us. "He'll be up and around in a few moments."

Alan and I exchange a knowing glance. These people want Henry's owners present for his journey to lucidity. I can't say I blame them, and I appreciate their concern for him.

"We're here, Henry. Time to get up." I scritch-scratch his chin.

His ears give a half-perk.

Jacob squats near him. "Want to go for a ride?"

Essence of Henry seeps into the dog's eyes. He climbs to his feet and staggers, three-legged, in a drunken circle, crashing his giant cone against everything in sight.

"He's not putting any weight on his front leg," I say, ignoring Henry's crazed smashing that's threatening to knock us all over like bowling pins.

The tech ignores it too. "He's pretty sore right now. That's normal."

Henry topples over.

I lunge toward him, wanting nothing more than to get him out of here as quickly as possible. I take advantage of his temporary immobility to snap on his leash.

Henry perks again. Leash means walk. Even on three legs, "walk" is good. He struggles to his feet and wobbles after us, whereupon he finally discovers this scary plastic thing around his face that makes noises when he moves. His totter jerks with panic, but the drugs prohibit any organized attack.

As we pass the rows of sick animals, a plaintive "*quack . . . quack*" wafts to my ears. Henry doesn't even notice.

Outside, we try to keep him from ramming every parked car in the lot (amazingly crowded for midnight). Even with our help, it takes two tries to get his cone head into our van. Hoping to bring Henry some comfort, I ride in the back with him.

He bashes against the front seats, turns, and finally discovers me sitting behind him. Dropping his backside to the floor, he plops his head upon my lap. His pleading "Save-me-my-head-is-trapped" eyes gaze up at me, then roll into the back of his head.

His chin slides off my lap as his body melts.

Thunk.

The dog hits the floor. Sound asleep in midair.

Except upon smacking the solid surface, he startles to alert mode, rediscovers the big scary thing around his face, and frantically searches for me once again.

Ah. There I am. He puts his rump to the floor, chin to my lap (frightening plastic thingy and all), and gives me the gaze, "Help me, help me . . . help . . . ."

Thunk.

Henry, the narcoleptic dog.

I try to get him to stay down on the floor, but he shoots up, does a three-legged spin, bashes the front seat, ricochets off the backseat, then twists and finally finds me.

Rump to floor, chin to my lap, "Help me" eyes going . . . going . . .

Thunk.

Really, this is getting serious. He tries so hard to sit, but his body crumbles every time he falls asleep, and I can't reach around the cone to prop him up.

He pulls himself up yet again.

"Stay down, Henry. Just stay down."

Nothing doing.

Thunk.

It's a long ride home.

At some point, thank God, sheer exhaustion keeps Henry on the floor. By the time we arrive home and open the van door, he's ready for another round of run-from-the-plastic-thingy. Furthermore, he needs to pee, which he can't seem to initiate on three legs with an anesthesia hangover.

In an erratic serpentine, he criss-crosses the yard. I trail, arms flailing, as if I can somehow help him pee or free him from cone phobia. Then he topples sideways and just lies there, sides heaving, tongue dangling.

After a few moments, he lifts a leg and pees into the air.

I scamper out of range. At least he found a way to empty his bladder.

"Good piddles, Henry. Good boy."

When he runs dry, I come close and whisper, "Come on, Henry. Let's go to bed."

His eyes glimmer recognition. Bed. Safe. Warm. He likes it there.

His inner homing device leads him to his crate. He bashes the opening with the cone, but his nearly shut-down body barely notices. I guide him in, and down he goes.

Alan comes into the room. "You think one of us should stay with him tonight?"

"Yeah, I'll do it. I doubt I'd get any sleep right now anyway."

Alan doesn't argue. We both know he has the gift of sleeping, whereas I have the gift of insomnia.

I lodge myself on the couch near Henry's crate and lie awake through the night, listening to him breathe.

At 4:30 a.m., he wakes, moves his head, and bashes the giant cone against the crate. The unexpected clamor rockets terror through him. I hear his body twist, and his breath heaves in panic.

That does it. I've had it with the cone thingy. I hop up and snatch the plastic nightmare off before Henry totally loses his mind.

"It's all gone, Henry. No more cone. No more noises. But you've got to leave your wound alone."

I figure he'll go back to sleep, but instead, he trembles and whimpers.

I dig out the bottle of pain medication the vet gave us. Henry had a dose earlier, but he clearly needs another. I squint my bleary eyes at the bottle. It takes five full seconds before I realize I can't read by moonlight. I flip on the lamp and squint some more.

Give once per day? As in, every twenty-four hours? Are they kidding?

I know my dog. He's a Rambo on the scale of pain tolerance. (I, on the other hand, am somewhere around The Princess and the Pea.) This dog hurts.

I snatch the phone, dial the all-night clinic, and explain my dog's needs.

"Well . . ." I hear a definite frown in the tech's voice. "Once per day really ought to be enough."

"Right, but he's trembling and whimpering. I know he's in a lot of pain."

"I can ask the doctor."

"Please."

I rub Henry's back and wish I could make the hurt go away.

The tech comes on the line. "Okay, the doctor says he can have some Tramadol. It'll be at the front desk for you."

That's the good news.

The bad news is that due to the risk of Henry licking, digging, or chewing his wound, I can't leave him unsupervised. He either needs to wear the horrible cone of terror, or I have to wake up Alan to go get the drug.

Poor Alan. He never had a chance with that one. When he sees Henry's portrayal of "Impressionistic Clichés: Shaking Like a Leaf," he heads straight for the clinic.

When Alan gets back, we can't get a pill down Henry's throat fast enough. I allow myself a small satisfied sigh. The drug will kick in soon.

I wait and watch for signs of improvement.

Surely he'll get more comfortable.

Anytime now.

I wring my hands.

I check the clock.

I count the seconds.

Henry remains fitful, trembling, dozing, and waking in a repeating cycle. I lie on the floor next to his open crate, with my arm reaching in to touch him. Normally I don't intrude into his den like that. It's his inner sanctum. But I can't help giving what small you're-not-alone comfort I can. More important, if I somehow doze off, I'll know if he wakes up and starts messing with his sutures. No way do we want a repeat visit to the vet.

At 10:00 a.m., I call the office again. "My dog, Henry, had sutures under anesthesia late last night and he's still in a lot of pain. He's had Deramaxx and Tramadol, but they're not helping. Can we give him something more?"

I can almost hear the tech's eyebrows rise. "Well, that really should be suitable."

"Right. But he's still trembling. Could you please ask the vet what else he can have?"

"I don't think she can give him anything more."

"Would you please check?"

Okay, so maybe I do have a note of desperation in my voice. You can argue that my Princess-and-the-Pea pain threshold over-empathized with Henry. But I don't really care.

She sticks me on hold for a while, then returns, her voice a tight line. "I'm sorry. We can't give him anything more."

"But—"

"That's all he can have. I'm sorry. Is there anything else you need?"

I bristle at her crisp tone. I need my dog to feel better. Why else would I call? With effort, I bite back the rude reply. She's just doing her job. "No . . . thanks."

"Have a nice day." She hangs up so quickly I almost miss her last word.

Then I remember my sister, who works in a doctor's office and regularly gets calls from drug-addicted patients with ludicrous excuses for extra refills on their prescriptions.

Yikes. Are they making a note in Henry's chart at this very moment? *Suspicious owner. Do not prescribe narcotics.*

I look at Henry. "They think I'm a junkie."

Then I stroke his trembling fur. "Or maybe, just maybe, you've had all the meds you can safely take. We'll have to wait it out."

We pass the long day side by side. I take breaks when Alan, Jacob, or Jonathan come to watch him. We tiptoe around the house, trying not to wake or startle him. He hurts least when he's asleep.

Once or twice he gets up to urinate, always hobbling on three legs. At least he figures out how to do it without falling over. But we can't help wondering, will this be permanent? How much damage did he do to his muscle? His nerves?

I spend another night alongside his crate. There's no choice. I can't bring myself to put the cone of terror back on this dog.

By Sunday, Henry's trembles disappear. Monday he puts weight on his leg. His recheck with the vet goes well. The sutures hold, the skin hasn't torn, the wound is healing.

God bless that woman's surgical skill.

I, on the other hand, am slowly turning into a blithering, sleep-deprived idiot. We have to do something about Henry's horrible cone phobia. I ask the vet's office if they have anything different.

They don't. But someone mentions a type of inflatable collar.

Hmm. It could work. Of course, at this point, chain mail would sound reasonable too.

Alan and I go on a mission: find a pacifistic collar before Erin loses her marbles. We accomplish our goal at the third pet store, a mere fifteen miles away. A blue inner tube that hooks to Henry's collar. My unfocused insomnia eyes don't even see the price tag.

Until later.

Thirty dollars? For an inner tube around the dog's neck?

Cha-ching.

At least I can sleep.

After five more days of recovery, Henry's leg looks good. Hallelujah for the upside of healing. I had a life before this window escapade, and I want it back. I miss little things like being able to go to the grocery store and church without a doggie sitter.

You might think that's a little paranoid, but consider the dog. We don't trust him for nothin'. If he can bite a hole through soccer balls, basketballs, and footballs, well, the thirty-dollar inner tube doesn't stand much chance. He's not supposed to be able to reach it with his teeth, but Henry defies all odds.

The downside of Henry's healing? His playful self wakes from its coma, and trying to keep him from pogoing around on a fragile, sutured leg becomes our new problem.

We count the days until his stitches can come out.

Early one morning, I think I hear a whimper, and when I open his crate door, he doesn't get up. I go wake the kids for school. When I return, Henry stands, but totters on three legs and keeps his injured leg curled up.

He stares at me through sad eyes.

He completed his antibiotics and was doing well without pain medication. Maybe he slept on it wrong? Morning stiffness? He's practicing to play himself in a movie someday?

After three hours, he fares no better.

I call the clinic. They tell me to bring him in the evening when the vet who fixed his leg would be there. Then I give him a dose of pain medication. Why not? We have them, and he's obviously in pain.

It doesn't help.

He spends the day hobbling, never putting an ounce of weight on his injured leg. He pretty much just wants to lie at my feet all day—weird for Henry.

I try to stay where he can be near me, but at one point I have to go upstairs to print out some documents. Unfortunately, it takes longer than I planned. I look up, and here comes Henry. His curiosity radar likely honed in on my stapler—small, squeaky, shoots pointy objects. The quintessential Siren song.

An ache seeps into my chest. He climbed all those steps on three legs. Worse, I'm about to head back downstairs where the rest of my work waits.

Now we have a problem. The poor dog stands at the top of the stairs—silly life preserver and all—trying to figure out how to get down. He can't lower his head well enough to see the stairs in front of him, but he knows they're there.

I see the *"Hmm"* go through his mind. His face droops in an "I really can't cope with this problem" look.

I don't see me successfully hauling sixty-five pounds of injured dog and inner tube down a steep flight of stairs, but I can't leave him up here all alone.

Unfortunately, I need to be downstairs to finish my work. I take the only option left. I go down a step, turn, hold out my arms, and brace myself to catch him if he falls.

Right. As if he won't just bowl me over, sending us both down in a tangled tumble, ending with a spectacular crash against the wall at the foot of the stairs.

With that picture in my head, I try to muster some enthusiasm. "Come on, Henry. Let's go downstairs."

He gives me his best "You're kidding" look.

"Sorry, buddy, I have to work downstairs. I'll walk you down."

He replies with his "That's the best you've got?" look.

"You can do it, Henry. I won't let you fall." Probably.

Next comes an "I don't like this at all" look. His gaze flits left and right as if another path will magically appear.

"You can't stay up here forever. Your food, your bed, your toys? All downstairs. And sooner or later you're going to need to piddle." Then I lower my voice. "We'll do it together."

He shifts his weight, rolls his eyes, and flashes his "Okay, I'll trust you, but I'm not going to like it" look. Then he steps off the edge of his world.

I tense, brace.

He doesn't fall. He looks left and right, then lurches off another step.

I move down and brace.

Step. Brace. Step. Brace.

Why do we have such a long staircase in this house?

"Good boy, Henry. We're almost there." We aren't, but it's not like he can count.

Step. Brace. Step. Brace.

He lands every blind step on one front leg. I sneak a peek behind me at the crushingly solid wall.

Step. Brace. Step. Brace.

"Almost there." And this time we really are almost there. We only need some imaginary background music to crescendo and we'll hit the bottom stair.

Step. Brace. Step. Brace.

My feet touch the wood floor. "We did it, Henry!"

He graces me with a cool look that says, "Don't think I'm forgetting this whole fiasco was your fault for going upstairs."

Yeah, just a little guilt there. I go straight to the fridge and bust out a big piece of cheese. There's no trauma known to dogs that a hunk of yellow moldy stuff can't cure.

The three-legged hobble remains, however. By evening, I can't wait to get him to the vet. Except the trip comes with a bit of a problem. Alan drove the junky, who-cares-if-you-bleed-in-it van to work, and he isn't home yet. That leaves me with the nice, we-don't-want-Henry-fouling-it-up car.

Naturally, Henry has to find a way to foul it up, so he spends the whole drive doing laps around the interior, slobbering everywhere and clawing his overgrown toenails into the leather seat. Whatever happened to Henry's three-legged lurch?

By the time we get to the clinic, he practically drags me in.

"My dog seems to have reinjured his leg," I explain to the receptionist's raised eyebrows.

Charisma Dog prances around making friends with the entire waiting room.

Nothing beats looking like a hypochondriac pet owner.

When his turn comes to go to the treatment room, he barely limps every eight steps. Once there, I try to ignore the jolly time Henry's having sticking his nose to every cabinet, drawer, and spellbinding table leg in the room.

I face the vet and paste on my best I'm-not-an-idiot look. "Umm, he's been hobbling on three legs and drooping in pain all day . . . except now . . ."

Without a hint of a snicker, the vet is kind enough to give Henry a thorough exam. She even decides to put him back on antibiotics and an anti-inflammatory drug, so I'm glad I brought him in.

Except I walk out of there minus eighty bucks and a fair chunk of dignity.

And I have to go back in two days to get the stitches out.

Maybe I'll send Alan.

Things never work out the way I plan. Of course I'm the one stuck lugging Henry back to the clinic.

His enchantment with the vet's office ends during stitch removal time, but they don't charge me extra for the fuss.

His battle scar shines as proof that he tackled the window, even as all traces of his limp fade. Naturally, we don't think he learned a thing. We park every patio chair we own, and even a table, in a straight line in front of the windows to defend against future assaults. If you ever come to my house, I trust you'll have the courtesy not to giggle at our furniture arrangement.

19

I finally trained Henry to walk nicely beside me. Really.

Not that I don't have to make frequent corrections—that's the nature of Henry. But for the most part, we can take a comfortable stroll with a loose leash.

Until Sweat-Suit Guy comes along. He's a nice man clad in black sweats who always seems to take his run while I'm out with Henry. At our first meeting, the man gives us a friendly wave and a cheery hello. Henry inexplicably responds with a barking tantrum.

How embarrassing. I do a horrible job reacting, which doesn't help. Next time I'll be prepared for his misbehavior, act more quickly, and get him under control.

Not.

But you'd think after several encounters, Henry would get used to the guy and lighten up.

Not.

I correct him endlessly, but Henry ignores my yanks. I command him to lie down, and I drag his chin to the ground. Then I step on his leash and force him to stay.

Not.

I don't have the weight to anchor him, and the pinch collar doesn't have enough sting to deter him. He scrambles, coughs, gasps, whines, and barks, creating one wingding of a scene. Then he's right back on his feet, and we do it all over again.

Sweat-Suit Guy avoids even looking at us these days.

Once he's well past us, Henry always resumes our placid stroll as if nothing horrible ever occurred in his entire lifetime.

My dog is bipolar.

I'm used to his outbursts while he's in our house, and we're working on curbing that. But on a walk? New problem.

It forces Alan and me to rethink the boys' Henry-walks. Since Jonathan doesn't have the mass or temperament to control Henry if he decides to create a ruckus, we opt to end their outings together.

Jacob's growth spurts allow him to continue his Henry-walks. What he lacks in experience controlling Henry, he makes up for in leverage. Still, we keep his time to the early afternoon, before the elementary school bus dumps its pillaging horde.

For variety, we also change Jacob's walk to a sprint around the entire block. Better Jacob than me on that sprinting detail, I guess, but I wish owning Henry didn't have to be like this.

Yet there are times when Henry morphs back into cutesy-puppy, bounding around the house playing hide-and-seek with Jonathan. As my son waits in some secret spot, holding a treat for him, Henry romps from hiding place to hiding place like the dog version of a giggling toddler. You can't watch that without smiling. His pure joy and happy-go-lucky demeanor make me think I only imagine his fits, like a bad dream remembered too vividly.

Then there are times when the boys are sick, lying miserable in their beds, and Henry wanders in, gives them a sniff, a tail wiggle, a sideways look from his velvety face. He changes everything for them at that moment. They call him close, stroke his fur, and hurt just a little bit less.

And then there's the unexpected bonus we discover when Henry and Jonathan spend more time on indoor play in exchange for their outdoor walks: Our kid has a talent for teaching Henry tricks, and wonder of wonders, Henry's capable of learning. Within a few short sessions, Henry grasps the intricacies of playing dead.

I know. Not a high-IQ feat. But sitting still has always been one of Henry's fundamental disabilities.

Soon he's also rolling over, begging, shaking hands, standing on his hind legs, catching a treat he tosses off his nose, and performing a host of other goofy gags a boy can invent. All for treats. Henry has stupendous focus when treats are involved.

One day I walk into the family room and find it transformed into a network of pillow tunnels.

Jonathan grins at me. "I'm teaching Henry to crawl."

Henry has that toddler-getting-a-cupcake twinkle in his eye. He dances in place as he watches Jonathan move to the other end of the tunnel.

Jonathan waves a treat and then ducks his head. "Crawl, Henry."

Henry plunks his belly to the carpet and crawls into the tunnel. My mouth drops open. G.I. Joe Dog lives at my house.

Halfway through the tunnel, Henry's rump pops through the pillow roof.

Jonathan dives farther into the tunnel like he can get Henry to copy him. "No, Henry. Crawl."

Henry bangs against a pillow holding up one side. It collapses, and the whole network topples like dominoes.

Through the mess, Henry scampers to Jonathan, his face one big grin of treat anticipation.

"You didn't crawl far enough, Henry."

His nose finds the treat in Jonathan's fist. He paws at it like he's trying to shake hands.

"No, you—"

He launches into a rollover. The pillows go flying.

"Henry, not—"

He sits up and begs.

"I didn't say—"

Dead dog.

"That's—"

He leaps from the dead and tries shaking hands again.

"All right, here."

Henry gobbles the little taste of heaven and sniffs for another.

Jonathan glances at me. "Well, at least he did the other ones right."

We both laugh, then he gathers the pillows and starts again.

For all our doorbell practices, the real event is unfortunately still a fail. Henry knows when People Who Don't Live Here wait outside. If familiar friends have come calling, we can eventually get him to relax. But today we have Girl Scouts, otherwise known as strangers.

The Scouts want to sell cookies. We want to buy cookies. Henry wants to bark maniacally at all trespassers whether they have cookies or not.

I drag our disturbed doggie into the nearest room and leave Alan and the boys to order the cookies.

Which means we'll be buying maybe sixty boxes.

If Henry's tantrum doesn't frighten the Scouts away.

He heads right for the windows and slams against them. For pity's sake, I don't need Cujo killing my cookie deal. I cram myself between my rampaging dog and the glass, then force Henry backward. In his frustration, he snaps at my hand.

I don't react quickly enough, and his teeth find skin.

My flesh tears, but I'm not mad or frightened, just determined as I tackle him. This is the best way to calm him.

He doesn't go down easily, but I'm used to that. I keep him pinned until the cookie transaction ends and the Girl Scouts leave. I hope somebody remembered Thin Mints are my favorite.

Henry couldn't care less about my cookie needs. In a weird sort of way, though, I'm coming to understand him better through these, er . . . bonding times, although I'm usually not bleeding through them.

Henry's chest stops heaving, but his eyes don't lose their panicky look. His whole face darkens with helplessness. Despair even. It digs into my heart and convinces me Henry doesn't *want* to be like this.

He just . . . is.

I hurt for him. For his broken instincts that make serenity so elusive. I can live with a gash on my hand. I know Henry's not trying to attack me or hurt me. But we can't have him losing his mind left and right. How deep does my responsibility to this dog go?

But abandoning him seems just as wrong. He's part of our family. We've been through so much, worked so hard. Could we really throw all that away? To truly give up on him—on anyone—is a horribly final thing.

Alan and I talk it over and arrange another house call with Angel. We meet outside for the ritual tinkle. When Henry's delirium dials down a notch, I fill Angel in on Henry's behavior.

"I should have gone to get his collar, but I really don't think it works right anymore."

Angel frowns. "You're keeping it tight?"

"Definitely. But it doesn't seem to give off much of a shock. Either that or it's just not strong enough."

"It's what, a couple of years old?"

"Nearly three, I think."

"These batteries don't last forever. In most cases, entry-level collars do fine. The dog gets trained and doesn't need a collar anymore."

"But in our case . . ."

Angel runs his hand down Henry's fur. "Maybe it's time to invest in a professional-level collar. We don't sell them at our store because they're really expensive, like five hundred bucks retail."

I look at dollar-sign doggie. *Cha-ching.*

"Let me check into it for you. Maybe I can get you a good deal from the guy who supplied mine."

"We have to do something. Henry was so whacked out at the window." My shoulders sag. "Sometimes I don't see how we'll ever get him past it."

"Training. Lots and lots of repetition. Henry's a tough dog."

"You don't think he's hopeless?"

Angel's face softens. "Difficult. Not hopeless. But there's no magic cure. Just lots of time. You need to do his exercises with him over and over and over. Even going back to the basic commands. Repetition helps obedience become automatic."

I think of the countless training hours we've already put into Henry. Not enough, apparently, because there's "repetition" where you do things lots and lots of times until you're blind with exhaustion and mind-numbingly bored, and then there's REPETITION— the kind that Henry requires that would eclipse the training regimen of an entire marine battalion.

Why, God, did we have to get a "difficult" dog? Some days I'd like to haul him right back to the breeder. Some days I think I might. But then there's that niggle—that stay-the-course whisper. It's ensconced somewhere inside me, and I'm stuck in this very hard place with this very hard dog.

20

Does it make me a bad person if I sometimes wish we hadn't gotten a dog? If I wish we could go back and pick a different one? If I feel duped by God?

Why didn't we get a lazy dog that gets fat and lolls at our feet all day? Why didn't we get a Mary Poppins dog that's sweet and cheery and loves everybody? I'd even take a brainless, compliant dog that lives to be a minion.

Instead, we got Henry.

There are still times I just want to be done with him.

I'm an ordinary person. I'm a mom and a wife. There are limits to my patience, my hope, and my ability to find any sort of coping skills, let alone enthusiasm, for the project known as Henry.

And what about my sons? Is Henry giving them a treasure trove of happy childhood memories?

Just when I feel my absolute rottenest over the boys getting stuck with this troublesome dog, they teach me something amazing about gratitude.

Early in our sons' lives, we started a ritual of bedtime prayers every evening. Being young, the boys' prayers were the simple, rote kind: "Dear Lord, thank you for this day. Thank you that I had fun. Help me to have no bad dreams tonight . . ."

Now that Henry has come along, they've changed the prayer.

"Dear Lord, thank you for Henry. Thank you that he's being good . . ."

Never mind that the only reason he's being good is that when he'd started his inevitable *barkbarkbark* routine as we'd gathered for prayer, Alan or I had grappled with him, forced him to the ground, and am, in fact, sitting on him at that very moment.

Even then, sometimes Henry wriggles free. The boys, though their eyes stay closed, can always hear the tussle, and then they change the prayer. "Dear Lord, thank you for Henry. Please help him to be good . . ."

They never fail to include the "thank you" in the prayer, though. Even if Henry had eaten one of their toys that day.

Thank you for Henry.

Even if they'd complained about having to watch him, or feed him, or help clean up his accidents.

Thank you for Henry.

Even if he'd hurt them by jumping, scratching, or falling on them. And let's face it, the dog's an ox on roller skates.

Thank you for Henry.

Every day. Every prayer.

Somewhere inside of me, a little hollow place gnaws into a bigger hollow place. *I* haven't been praying that prayer. I haven't been praying much of any prayer where Henry is concerned—well, except maybe why, why, *why*?

I expect to navigate through this mess, how? If there's one thing an ordinary person like me needs, it's the extraordinary strength I can find in God. What am I doing trying to go it alone?

Oh, for the childlike faith of my kids as I fail so miserably. They've hit on the key—their gratitude is a barb in my conscience.

Yet I struggle.

Thank you, God, for giving me a moronic, suicidal, disobedient, time-consuming wreck of a dog?

Just when I think Henry's headed for nothing but more worrisome behavior, he begins an odd new ritual at home. When I open his crate in the morning, instead of leaping out and barking like a mad dog, he yawns all leisurely-like, eases himself upright, and waltzes out of his little den. He bows in a lazy stretch, and then performs a head-to-toe, wake-up shimmy. After that, he strolls into the living room, sits, and looks at me. His eyes have that "I'm sitting so nicely don't you want to come pet me?" look.

I plant myself in front of him, rub his chest and face, and tell him what a good boy he is. After all, he isn't destroying anything or pogoing through the house.

His neck curves into a playful arch, and he puts his forehead to my chest, just below my neck, and rests it there.

Is our aloof little doggie demonstrating some actual attachment?

What starts as a once or twice fluke turns into a semi-regular occurrence, not just with me but with Alan and the boys too. I call it a Henry Hug. It keeps us going, trying, hanging in there with this impossible dog. Like he's reaching out, wanting to be normal.

21

The sadly necessary, new shock collar (*cha-ching*) arrives, but through a different source than expected. My dad—I believe I mentioned he knows half the population of Missouri—hooks us up with a deal.

The collar feels thick and strong. No-nonsense all the way. I read the directions and get it charged. Then comes time for a trial run.

I wimp.

It's a hesitation born in part from being out of the habit of using a shocker, and in part because I know what that shock feels like, based on the neurological test I'd had. It grieves me that Henry needs this kind of training.

I mention this to a cattle rancher friend of mine.

"As someone whose livelihood comes from animals," she tells me, "I think they have to be controlled or they're no good to anyone. Not even themselves."

"But I hate the harshness of the shock."

"We use miles and miles of electric fences. Every now and then I get knocked to the ground by accidentally touching the wire, and nobody worries about that."

All righty then. If my friend can handle a shock dumping her on her behind, maybe I shouldn't feel so guilty.

Later that day, I pull the collar out of the box and scan the number of shock levels.

Fifty. As in, five-zero.

Is the thing made for elephants?

I set it to the first level—Chihuahua setting. Or maybe gerbil. A tingly buzz rather than pain. We may need a higher setting at some point, but the directions say to start with level one.

For the next two days, Henry wears the collar periodically in the house.

Behavior much improved.

I still don't get why it has fifty levels, though.

By the third day, level one no longer cuts it.

We kick the setting up a notch. Behavior modified.

That evening, as Alan and I are getting ready to walk Henry, I pick up the shock collar. "What do you think about using this instead of the pinch collar on Henry? His behavior on walks keeps getting worse."

Alan tugs on the shock collar's metal ring. "It feels sturdy enough, as long as Henry doesn't pull a lot."

"If he pulls . . . " I nod at the zapper.

We hook Henry up and head for the garage door. Doubts worm into my thoughts. What if the leash clasp fails and Henry breaks loose? What if the collar tears? What if he freaks out because he doesn't know how to react without the pinch collar?

I give Alan a tight smile. "Here goes nothing."

We step outside.

Henry doesn't feel his normal pinch collar around his neck.

FREEDOM!

Zoom.

Zap.

"Ouch," says his head-ducked, tail-tucked body language. "Maybe if I go the other way," says his instinctive compulsion.

Zoom.

Zap.

"Ouch." The tail tucks farther, the head ducks lower. "I'll try a different way."

Zoom.

Zap.

"Ouch." He runs to me and positions himself in the proper heel position.

I give him a reassuring rub down his side. "Good foose, Henry. That's a good foose."

Henry's nub of a tail glues down to his rump, and his ears shrink back against his head. With his chin hanging all of six inches off the ground and his legs perpetually bent in a half crouch, we head for the trail and proceed around the neighborhood lake. Whenever Henry leaves my side, I repeat the foose command and hit the button.

It's not a fun walk.

The instruction book says that with encouragement and patience, your dog will catch on to the training method and learn to react confidently.

I hope so.

We try again the next day and don't get on much better.

By the third walk, Henry's head pops up now and again, and his tail hangs in neutral.

Encouraging progress, but I also have to use level three a few times.

The following day, we meet up with the dreaded enemy of enemies. The end-all of evil. The despicable, plague-carrying, territory-usurping paragon of all iniquity.

The mail truck.

Henry snaps. Raving, hurl-himself-at-a-large-moving-vehicle hysteria.

This behavior has to stop.

Zaaap.

Level three has zero effect. I'm not surprised. Henry's mind has gone to a place normal methods of correction can't reach. But this collar has a button for just such an occasion. It's called Rise. To be used in emergencies.

This is a bona fide, flipped-out emergency.

"Phooey!" I hold down the Rise button. As long as I press it, the shock setting continues to increase.

With a loud yelp, Henry snaps out of berserk mode somewhere around level eight or nine. His rump hits the pavement in an immediate sit. His head swivels, and he actually looks at me, gives me his entire attention span.

His yelp echoes in my ears and makes my insides shrivel. I hate that I've had to shock him into behaving, but I force my voice into a happy sound. "Good *sitz*, Henry."

The mail truck zips past.

Henry remains in surrender mode.

Not only that, he almost seems, well, relaxed. As if the burden of having to tear up the mail truck evaporated. I see normality come over him. A sense of freedom from the stress of challenging every noisy vehicle that comes down the road. It's a glimpse of Henry as he should be.

I never planned on having a "difficult" dog who'd need tirades trained out of him this way. Does anyone? But I can't argue with the change in Henry's behavior.

The next time we walk during mail truck time, we have to replay the ugly zapping ritual.

The results are the same. Obedience after pain. I try lower levels, but only the yowl setting can knock him out of his frenzy. This dog's stubborn streak runs ten miles long and five wide.

Angel warned us Henry's training demanded repetition. Lots.

Day after day. Week after week.

And nobody ever said it would be easy.

Uncomfortable truth number two: I live under a rock of naïveté where I think discipline is tidy, simple, and noncontroversial. Wrong.

Discipline is messy.

22

The passing months (and months) of shock-collar training continue to rehabilitate Henry. We go out on the neighborhood trail every day. Dirt bikes, dog walkers, delivery trucks—we safely navigate them all. I use the Rise button less and less, then it becomes a thing of the past. Not that I don't need to pay attention and be sure Henry knows I mean business. But that's what he's always needed—a strong (as in titanium) hand.

Those same months bring positive changes within our house too. Henry's come a long way from our wrestling matches, where I'd have to drag, push, or otherwise coerce him away from the windows and then pin him to the ground. If I let him up, he'd zoom right back to the windows. Again and again and again and again and again.

And again.

And then some more.

No, I am not exaggerating.

Portions of this book were written while I sat on my living room floor, pinning the stupid dog under my legs. Sometimes he seemed to actually like being pinned, but it made typing hard.

Fortunately, it finally occurs to Alan and me that we can block Henry's approach to the front windows by using a gate left over from our kids' baby days. Henry can leap the gate if he wants to, but the dog who'll take on a mail truck and not think twice (or even once) is afraid of the gate. I can't explain that. I know it fell over a couple of times and made a racket, but really? That's going to stop him from going near the thing for the rest of his life?

Apparently.

That leaves him only one more set of street-view windows to jump against—the kitchen ones. We fix this by copying the oh-so-elegant pattern on the patio—we block the kitchen windows with four lined-up chairs. Another stunning furniture arrangement that belongs on the cover of *House Ridiculous*.

Even if Henry can't jump against the windows anymore, he still likes to pitch a fit next to them. But the new collar, which has yet to malfunction, helps us establish a training routine. I work in the living room every morning and keep the zapper handy. When some noisy truck rumbles by, a zap interrupts Henry's stampede toward the windows. With low level zaps, I force Henry to heel, walk him to his blankie, and make him lie down.

I can't turn my back, or he'll sneak over to the windows again.

We repeat this ritual so many times, with so many zaps, that one day he actually comes without the zapper at all. I about lose my eyeballs out my head.

"Good boy, Henry! You came. Good foose!"

I walk him to his blankie. Dare I try for more when he isn't currently collared?

You betcha. "Sitz, Henry."

He looks at me as if the command to sit doesn't mean he actually has to sit.

I move my body closer, crowding him against the wall.

He tries to scoot aside.

I move closer yet, then park my fists on my hips in my best I-mean-business pose.

He eyes me for a moment or two, then gives me a grudging, "Oh all *right*" look. His tush touches down.

"Good sitz. Now platz."

He turns his head.

I crowd him again and put my finger to his blankie.

Nothing.

I hold my pose.

He inches his body to the floor, but deliberately avoids landing on his blankie.

My dog is passive-aggressive.

I still have to praise him for lying down, though. "Good platz, you stinker. Now, blibe."

Yeah, he stays. So long as I stay too.

Amazingly, this process starts shutting down the *barkbarkbark* routine. I simply have to call him to heel, walk him to his blankie, intimidate him into lying down, and stand there guarding him.

Over and over, day after day, endlessly repeating the motions.

Exhausting, but exhilarating too. This process is working. Henry obeys.

Even without the zapper.

Here's a weird thing. I go to my folks' house for a few days to enjoy my annual birthday visit. My sister meets me there, and we hang out without any children or husbands or pets. Our parents spoil us, and we eat fattening food, shop for hours, fish, cruise in the boat, and goof around. Dream vacation.

Sometime during the visit, a little flicker of loss wiggles through my psyche. Right in the middle of some conversation we're having about my sister's African grey parrot. (Nadine hasn't lost her fondness for pets.) My flicker feels disturbingly like a teensy longing for my doggie.

Surely I just don't know what to do with myself without outlandish Henry problems sucking up all my time.

Some months later, I'm heading off for a writers' conference. I adore going to these things—seeing old friends, making new friends, learning about writing.

But I despise traveling *to* them. It usually involves an airplane, and I'm not good with airplanes. Nothing short of a giant, national-level writers' conference could induce me to risk crash-landing in a fiery heap.

Scratch that. The conference alone doesn't cut it.

But the more I pray about it, the more I feel God's nudge. And that *will* get me off the ground in a hunk of metal.

Consequently, I'm gathering my suitcase and laptop and taking a final look around the house for anything I've forgotten. And yes, it goes through my mind that it just might be my very last look around the house ever.

I'm so melodramatic. But I'd be lying if I denied it.

When those thoughts come, I usually swallow hard and remind myself that God is in control, and what he wills, will be.

Alan gives me a sympathetic grin. He knows how I feel about planes. "Are you ready to go? We need time to park so I can help you get your bags into the terminal."

"Let me take care of Henry." By that, I mean do the official put-Henry-in-his-crate-because-he's-not-going-in-the-C-A-R routine. It's not until after I've slid the crate's bolts in place that a pang hits me.

Longing.

Sadness.

I hadn't given Henry a good-bye pet.

Then again, I'm not in the habit of doing so. I'm usually just going to the grocery store, not getting on a plane that could fall out of the sky.

I look at Henry's silky fur, so inviting. I hadn't run my hand along his side, and now I want to. What if I never see him again?

Alan stands at the garage door. "Let's go."

There's no fixing it. If I open the crate, Henry will shoot to the door and begin his "Yippee, I'm going for a ride" dance.

And no, he can't go. His territorial issues include our vehicles, so we can't leave him alone in the car. It wouldn't do to have him crash through the windshield because some sparrow trots across the hood.

I turn from the crate and troop out of the room.

Heading for my possible doom.

Or maybe just a smooth flight that gets me where I need to go and gives me a more thankful attitude for aeronautical engineering.

Between prayers for mechanical safety and pilot skill, I sit on the plane and ponder that pang. After four years, do I finally have some semblance of attachment for my nutcase dog?

23

Henry's black muzzle started to gray sometime around his third birthday. Maybe sooner. Now, just shy of five years old, a raccoon-ish, salt-and-pepper routine decorates his face. Personally, I think it's because he's living the life of three dogs at once, and it's finally burning him out.

Case in point, I'm lying on my bed reading this evening, and he wanders into the room, plunks down on the floor between my bed and the window, and just lies there.

Normally this spot is reserved for his backyard bunny vigil. But today he's not even looking outside. It's like he's content to just hang out.

Jacob comes in a few minutes later. "Oh, there's Henry. I wondered where he went." Even at this age, we still have to protect Henry from lethal stupidity.

Henry looks up and gives a tail wiggle.

Jacob runs a hand over Henry's fur. "You know, I think he's calming down some. Turning into a good dog, even."

I love Jacob's optimism. I suppose he's always had it, but I've just never taken it to heart. He's right, though. Now that Henry's barking tirades are more under control, and he's finally exhibiting signs of energy depletion, and showing more interest in our companionship, maybe he really could become a good dog. I mean, if he doesn't kill himself first.

My phone rings. It's Alan. "Jonathan and I had some time to kill before his rehearsal, so we're at PetSmart."

I can already hear a *cha-ching*.

"Jonathan wants to get a new toy for Henry. A tuggy rope. What do you think?"

Aside from the fact that we already have a tuggy rope? "If you're going to buy something, he could use a much bigger Kong. His is puppy-size."

"I didn't think he liked that toy."

"He doesn't—not to play with. But he loves to lick peanut butter out of it. Except it only holds a little bit."

Read: Giant Kong plus more peanut butter equals dog occupied for more than two minutes.

"I'll see what I can find." He hangs up.

It's nearly midnight when they return from Jonathan's show. Theater is for people who don't do mornings.

The second they walk in, Henry homes in on new rubber. It releases pheromones or something. He bounces to Jonathan, eyes shiny with toy delirium.

Jonathan looks at me. "Can I give it to him?"

My bleary eyes plead for bedtime, but logic says Henry can't be turned off now. Better to let him have the toy. He'll chomp on it a few minutes, realize there's no peanut butter, and toddle off to bed.

"All right."

Jonathan tries to rip the Kong from its cardboard packaging, but it's locked in with sturdy plastic ties. The struggle ratchets up Henry's gotta-have-it excitement. Jonathan twists left and right, trying to avoid Henry, and yanks away at the plastic.

He still can't break out the goods. Is the package designer former Delta Force or what?

"You try." Jonathan performs a covert handoff to me.

Doesn't fool the dog. His nose finds TOY, and he jitterbugs through the kitchen after me. The free-the-Kong-from-the-package operation calls for bolt cutters or something, but I'm improvising with the closest thing at hand—a large pair of scissors.

I hack away at the zip ties and finally release the toy. I think the scissors might be a casualty of war, though.

Jonathan takes the Kong and heads for the living room. Henry trounces after him.

Sure, Jonathan gets to play the hero. He hands it over, and Henry peels through the house, chomping his toy.

"You better get ready for bed, Jonathan. It's late."

"But I'm watching Henry. He's so cute with his toy."

"I know, but he won't play long. There's no peanut butter."

Fifteen minutes later, the whole family is ready for bed, and Henry still blazes through the house, chomping, chasing, chewing, and possibly even chortling.

Alan watches Henry zoom past. "What should we do?"

"What if you take him out for his last piddles while I'll steal his toy."

Alan shoots me a raised-brow look.

I shrug. "It's late. He'll probably forget about it and go right to his crate for bed. He doesn't really like Kongs without peanut butter."

With a load of persuasion, Alan gets Henry to drop the Kong for a trip out the back door. I swipe the toy and stuff it in a laundry room cabinet.

When Henry comes in, he doesn't head to his crate at all. Instead, he dashes straight to the Kong's last known whereabouts and stands there all saggy-faced and tragic. His wrinkly forehead says, "My toy . . . oh, my toy . . ."

Then he runs around the house sniffing for rubber.

"Henry, let's get a treat and go to bed." Alan heads for the goodie stash.

Henry does an immediate U-turn. A treat clearly ranks higher than his long-lost toy. He gallops into his crate, munches his snicky-snack, and settles down.

The rest of us head for our pillows, and the house goes to lights-out status. Five minutes later, I'm cozy and dozy under my blankets.

A lonely little whine wafts from the back room. Then another. And another.

I pretend I don't hear it.

Whine. Whine. Whine. Whine. Whine. Whine.

Okay, I hear it, but I don't care.

WhineWhineWhineWhineWhineWhineWhineWhine.

Now I have to care because it feels like a needle going through my head. "What is that dog's problem?"

Alan groans. "You think he still wants the toy?"

"But he doesn't even like Kongs. Surely he's forgotten about it?"

The whining turns into wailing sounds.

I roll over, but it doesn't help the stabbing needle thing. "Maybe he didn't finish his business outside."

"He was out there a long time."

Twelve annoying minutes later, Alan throws off the covers, stomps to Henry's crate, and puts him through the whole bed-time routine again—out, treat, back in the crate. Henry gets a little distracted wanting to sniff through the house, but the treat does its work.

The clock reads 1:00 a.m. by the time Alan climbs back into bed. We have seven blissful minutes of silence. Then a doggie moan grinds out long and slow, as if Henry was marooned on some desolate island hundreds of miles from the nearest hint of food, friend, or squeaky toy.

I shake my head. "He won't keep it up long."

"He's gotta be tired."

Half an hour later, my nerves are so raw I think they're bleeding. How can Henry still whine about that hunk of rubber? He has object permanence? Kongs really do give off pheromones?

Alan flops to his back. "Should we put the Kong in there with him?"

"Unsupervised?"

Henry can rip a hole through a thick squeaky ball in twenty minutes. Give an obsessed, aggressive chewer all night and who knows what he'd do. No way am I calling the vet tomorrow to confess my dog consumed an entire Kong.

Alan cocoons his head under his pillow. "I guess we wait it out."

The wailing train gathers steam and rolls on through the night.

By 3:00 a.m., the sanity I once had is a vague, happy memory. I stalk to Henry, yank open his crate, and bring him into our room so he can't keep waking the boys. But I refuse to give that dog his Kong. For sure he'd tear it into bitty pieces and gulp it down right after I have the gall to fall asleep.

Maybe being with us will distract him.

It does indeed. For thirty whole seconds.

Then he sniffs, snorts, lies down, gets up, paws at the carpet, wanders, whines, sighs, sulks, whimpers, and huffs.

Oh, for a tranquilizer gun.

After four solid hours of Kong obsession—does Guinness have a record for that?—Henry succumbs to a fitful sleep.

We look like wrecks the next day at church and feel worse. I want to stay angry with Henry, but I suppose he can't help it if he's neurotic. After a morning of worship, it's easier to forgive him, and I'm resigned—this is how life with Henry will always be.

At least we can make his day by finally giving him the Kong. I fish it out of the cabinet and head for the family room where the rest of my brood is gathered. Henry trails me so closely he steps on my heels. A little wave of gratification ripples through me as I present the Kong to Henry. He'll be ecstatically occupied all day, and our family will have the freedom to lie around like the sleep-deprived zombies we are.

Henry takes the toy, plops on the floor, and chews the Kong for possibly one whole minute. Then he up and walks away from it.

End of all-consuming passion.

For no apparent reason.

This is how life with Henry will also always be.

My gratification lies souring in my stomach, but before it can ferment into frustration, Henry ambles back into the family room. He circles slowly, like he's counting us all. Then he plunks down at my feet and takes a nap right there in the midst of us, as if we really are his people.

Maybe this is how life with Henry can be now too.

24

Rain always comes as a distasteful surprise to Henry. This morning is no different. He wakes up, eats his breakfast, and heads to the back door for a date with his bodily functions. He does the potty dance while I struggle with the lock. At the first crack of air, he bursts through the door.

His claws skid to a stop on the patio.

Major dilemma. He's gotta go. Bad.

But it's raining.

Which makes the bladder thing all the more uncomfortable.

He cowers on the edge of the cement, lifts his leg, and pees on the brick column supporting the roof.

Lovely. What are the chances it will rain sideways and wash the bricks so I don't have to trek out there with the hose?

Unfortunately, for those of us concerned about roundworms, tapeworms, and fecal coliform bacteria, Henry's only dealt with half his bodily functions.

He circles the patio and squats dead center.

Windblown rain will be no help there.

Henry doesn't even give me an "I'm sorry" look. He slithers into the house, shaking as if three raindrops could melt him.

After morning poop, it's normally time for our walk. I no sooner get the back door closed than Henry starts his yippee routine. He scampers through the house, leaping every few feet just in case I don't remember how much he wants to go out.

"Henry, it's raining."

He gives me that *letsgoletsgoletsgo* look. The one where he quivers head to toe, and his eyes sparkle like there's nothing behind his eyeballs but a giant Roman candle.

"Henry, you pooped on the patio, remember? It was raining so hard you wouldn't put a paw to the grass. If it's raining in the backyard, it's raining in the front too."

His big, dopey face stares expectantly at me.

"R-A-I-N."

No change on Dopey's features.

"It will be raining on the sidewalk, raining on the street, and raining on the trail. Raining, in fact, everywhere you want to walk."

He keys on the word *walk* and leaps again.

"We're not going." I turn away and pick up my laptop to work.

It takes him a while to absorb the situation. His happy feet go still. He gazes around the room. He walks to the door. Finally he starts whining.

I plop on the couch and shove my laptop open. Maybe I can tune out his whine-whine-whining.

Not.

"Quit it, already." I've got that needle-through-my-head thing again.

WhineWhineWhineWhineWhineWhineWhineWhine.

"I want to go too, but we can't. It's RAINING."

WhineWhineWhineWhineWhineWhineWhineWhine.

"Enough!"

Nice pair we make. He's whiney and I'm crabby. I mean, I look forward to my exercise every bit as much as this stupid dog.

Good grief, we have something in common. You all might've

215

figured that out by now, but me, not so much. I believe I've covered my shortcomings in the perpetual brilliance department.

All right. So we both like exercise, but that's as far as it goes. Or is it?

I'm not stubborn.

Not really.

Okay, maybe once in a while I can be, shall we say, willful?

I suppose I'll have to admit to a little single-mindedness at times. But that's where our similarities cease. I'm not neurotic.

Am I?

Good grief, with such flawed creatures running around, it's a wonder the world doesn't fall apart. Is there any hope for us?

Henry stands in front of me. His face droops in a mournful "Oh, why can't we walk?" look.

I sit on the floor and draw him closer. He plunks down, not entirely willingly. After all, if he sits, I might forget he wants to go out.

The rain batters our roof. I rub Henry's silky fur until his tension eases and he finally lies down.

"Good boy. Good platz."

My German is still lousy, but Henry sighs like he's resigned to some inexplicable delay of our walk. Clearly, he will never grasp the intricacies of rainfall ubiquity. Chalk up another wobble in Henry's loose screw.

I'm not really surprised, of course. After four years, this dog hasn't completely graduated from his shock collar, either. He likely never will. Nor has he outgrown his baffling, random fetishes, his propensity to swipe our dinner steaks, or his constant bumbling into mortal danger by, say, eating an expensive bottle of guitar polish.

This is who Henry is.

He sighs again, and nudges his warm body closer to mine. He does this more and more lately. Takes comfort, gives comfort. I lean into him and let my frustration ebb.

"I'm sad about the rain too, buddy."

He sticks his head on my lap, and his entire face fixes in a "Woe is us" pout only a boxer could conjure.

A twinge hits me. One of those leaving-on-an-airplane pangs. Then it turns into a flood that fairly well bowls me over. Yes, I feel sorry for Henry, but this is more than that.

I think about all we've been through together. The ridiculous adventures like near-death-by-scooter. The joys like reuniting the look-alike stray with her owner. The laughter when Henry romps through every trick he knows—except the correct one—to get a treat. The ache of nursing him back to health after he blew our window to smithereens. And even the long road of tempering his tantrums.

I know normality will never be an option with Henry. Sometimes I think his screw just might fall out. But suddenly there's this impossible new truth beating in my heart.

I *love* this dog.

Real actual feelings.

I don't know how this happened.

Or maybe I do.

Because maybe this is the sum of countless choices. Every decision I've made to keep going, keep working, keep trying has added up to loving Henry with my actions, even when my feelings were anything but.

Funny how the warmth of emotion caught up to my choices somewhere along the way. Like finding a rare gift in a beat-up box.

I'm not sure I believed it was possible, but this bond I have with Henry is a treasure—hammered gold, forged through the sweat and blood of every Henry-walk, every rescue from the lake, every training exercise repeated over and over and over. It's anchored in my heart more deeply than a childish affection, more concretely than my futile wish for Henry to be something he's not.

After four years of interminable trial, when all I was prepared for was an easy love like I had with my childhood boxer, I finally see the message that's been pouring like rain in the front yard, the backyard, and everywhere else.

Through Henry, God has been giving me not needless suffering, but a lesson in real love—God's love. The kind of love he has for me. The kind that's the hope for all of us flawed creatures.

Real love can't be about satisfying a feeling. It's too hard for that. It costs and it hurts and it's one life-wrenching mess of a lesson. It's choices and challenges and changes that are about you and not about the other person. It's embracing—no, *embodying*—the notion of unconditional giving. Of mercy. Of commitment.

It's becoming a better person for having lived through the crucible.

God did not punish me with a whacko dog. Henry is a gift. An opportunity day by day, minute by minute, disaster by disaster, to discover not what Henry can become, but what *I* can become.

I wouldn't trade this adventure for anything.

Maybe, after all is said and done, this isn't a dog's redemption story at all.

Maybe it's mine.

I believe I can mean it now. Thank you, God, for Henry.

Erin Taylor Young is a humor writer who works in a library where she gets to wander among books. She loves football, photography, and hiking in national parks. Erin has written for *Today's Christian Woman*, *Thriving Family*, and *MidWest Outdoors*. In 2013, she received a Higher Goals Award from the Evangelical Press Association. She was a finalist in the 2012 Genesis contest for her contemporary fiction. She lives in Oklahoma with her well-meaning husband, two polar-opposite sons, and a noncompliant dog. Find out more at www.erintayloryoung.com.

WANT MORE?

Visit **SurvivingHenry.com** to
learn more about the author
watch videos of Henry's crazy antics
and stay connected!

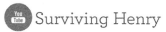 SurvivingHenry

Surviving Henry

**A wagging tail. A goofy, floppy-tongued smile.
An excited bark when your keys jingle in the door.**

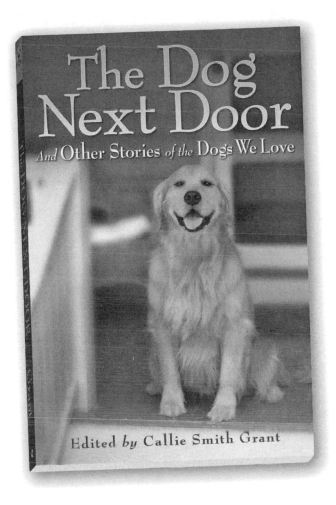

A heartwarming collection of true stories about the beautiful
relationship between people and their dogs.

Ⓡ Revell
a division of Baker Publishing Group
www.RevellBooks.com

**A playful bat of a string. A bored yawn.
A tender purr at the touch of your hand.**

A heartwarming collection of true stories about the
connections between humans and their cats.

The gut-bustingest, knee-slappingest, guffaw-inducingest collection of clean jokes you can find! COLLECT THEM ALL!

Q: *Why did the boy eat his homework?*
A: Because the teacher said it was a piece of cake.

Q: *What do you find at the end of everything?*
A: The letter "g."

Q: *What do you get when you cross a dentist and a boat?*
A: A tooth ferry.